*Seeking the Light of God's Comforter
When Challenges Dim Our View*

Seeking the Light of God's Comforter
When Challenges Dim Our View

Dick ♡
    Look what happened!
It took some time as all
God's best gifts often do.
I am happy to share this
gift copy with you as I
rejoice in God's favor.

                        Lynn
                        1/2017

Lynn L. Severance

REDEMPTION
PRESS

Published by Redemption Press, PO Box 427, Enumclaw, WA 98022
Toll Free (844) 2REDEEM (273-3336)

Redemption Press is honored to present this title in partnership with the author. The views expressed or implied in this work are those of the author. Redemption Press provides our imprint seal representing design excellence, creative content and high quality production.

ISBN 13: 978-1-63232-909-7 (Softcover)
      978-1-63232-917-2 (Hardcover)
      978-1-63232-918-9 (ePub)
      978-1-63232-920-2 (Mobi)

Library of Congress Catalog Card Number: 2016946815

TABLE OF CONTENTS

Section One
Hope—Faith—Redemption—Love—Praise

Section Two
Comfort—Goodness—Peace—Kindness—Flexibility

Section Three
Gratitude—Trust—Faithfulness—Abundance—Surrender

Section Four
Courage—Perseverance—Strength—Compassion—Incarnation

ENDORSEMENTS

Comfort is a God-given grace that can surprise and almost overtake us during the most painful and tumultuous times. Just when we are at our lowest; just when we've lost all hope, God sends relief through the consolation of an uplifting word, an inspiring image, an insightful question, and an encouraging remark. This is why I love Lynn Severance's new book, *Seeking the Light of God's Comforter—When Challenges Dim Our View.* Through photos, quotations, intuitive questions, and warm-hearted stories, Lynn helps the reader embrace the solace of the Holy Spirit. With every page, we find another reason to trust God through the toughest of times. I heartily recommend this special devotional book—something that will bolster every hurting heart!

—Joni Eareckson Tada
Joni and Friends International Disability Center
Agoura Hills, California

Lynn Severance is a woman of great courage. We read in the Scriptures how "He will give us the treasures of darkness; riches stored in secret places." Lynn's life is that treasure with riches stored in who she has become. Her work has preceded her already and "gone global"! When I was a concierge at HEAL AFRICA's hospital in the Congo DRC, people came from around the world to work with the least, the last, and the lost. We oftentimes read one of Lynn's devotionals around the breakfast table before we began another day at the hospital. Lives have been touched, hope restored, and destinies altered through her words. My late husband, Tim Hansel, believed in how his story connected to Lynn's story. His hope was that other readers would find HIS story therein, helping them to move forward in God's life-giving ways. As Lynn has surrendered to her chronic illness over the past thirty years, her life circumstances continue to be a servant of the gospel.

—Anastasia Hansel, MA, Global Leadership
Founder of Global Women in Leadership Network
Motivational Speaker and Adventure Coach
Dana Point, California

My friend Lynn Severance has the gift of encouragement, and you will experience her gift as you absorb this book. Lynn writes from a place of deep pain and even deeper faith. Her hard-won insights on Scripture and God will bless, comfort, and move those who have faced suffering and wondered why . . . and what's next. All of us experience affliction if we live long enough—some of us more than others. Chronic pain, loss of physical ability, even broken relationships are normal parts of the Christian walk, though we are tempted to think otherwise. *Seeking the Light of God's Comforter—When Challenges Dim Our View* doesn't sugarcoat this truth. It does, however, help us to discover the sweet presence of the Spirit amid the sometimes bitter circumstances of life. Highly recommended!

—Stan Guthrie, author
God's Story in 66 Verses:
Understand the Entire Bible by Focusing on Just One Verse in Each Book,
All That Jesus Asks: How His Questions Can Teach and Transform Us
Wheaton, Illinois

Lynn Severance shares her heart, passion, and faith journey in, *"Seeking the Light of God's Comforter—When Challenges Dim Our View*. As an optometrist, I have the joy of helping people daily with their vision. Lynn is a patient of mine with considerable visual challenges, yet recognizes God's vision in His gift of grace to persevere. Through Lynn's writing and photography, she opens the eyes of her readers to see God's word in a new way. She shares her perspective of how God's Comforter has changed her vision and how He can change yours, and that of others blinded by pain and trials. May God's grace and love be evident in your spiritual journey, as you are encouraged through His words, Lynn's photography, and the meditations in this book. Thank you, Lynn.

—Nancy G. Torgerson, OD, FCOVD
Alderwood Vision Therapy Center
Lynnwood, Washington

Lynn Severance and I met when she came on staff where I am a devotional writer for Rest Ministries, an online Christian website for those with chronic illness. As we got to know each other, I learned of the many life challenges she has faced with grace and a strong faith. I went from being inspired by her heartfelt writings to being inspired by her life itself. I believe that the comforting truths, so beautifully written, combined with Lynn's amazing photographs will provide the encouragement and inspiration she embodies. I'm grateful to be able to call her my friend, and even more grateful to have had the privilege to endorse her writing, as I am convinced they are words that many will glean quiet comfort from during their challenging days.

—deni hansen-gray weber, Psy/D, ET/P
licensed Indiana psychologist
professional educational therapist, retired
admin, Peace in Chronic Illness
mixed-media and pastel artist

What a convergence of authenticity and beauty is this grace-filled offering by Lynn Severance. Hope hallmarks every page as Lynn reflects on her own life experiences, particularly those of chronic and debilitating illness, and views them through the lens of expectant faith in a loving God. She is tried but not disappointed. Her faithfulness in persevering with the questions is surpassed only by God's faithfulness in providing the courage and comfort needed. All of this is gathered up and given as gift of beauty to the reader. Lynn chronicles her journey with the language of a sage/poet but also with the artistry of pictures that delight the eye and stir the heart. This book is a gift to all who walk the challenging path of seeking God's Light in difficult times.

—Kathleen MacInnis Kichline, MDiv
Author: *Sisters in Scripture, Never On Sunday,* and *Elders of the Bible*
adjunct faculty School of Theology and Ministry, Seattle University

In *Seeking the Light of God's Comforter—When Challenges Dim Our View,* Lynn comes beside those with chronic illness, which is not a temporary loss as it rips away hopes and plans. The gift of this book is that Lynn digs deeply into her own soul, facing the reality of permanent loss and then puts what she finds on paper. The reader feels Lynn's constant spark of hope. She never turns away from what is hard. She feels the fears, admits her fallibilities, and draws us closer to her. We are comforted that we have found someone willing to share the run-away emotions illness brings. Lynn is determined to not miss a word that the Holy Spirit whispers to her. Facing the upheavals takes time and energy we don't have. Lynn gives us a starting place through her words and stunning photography. I am eager to share Lynn's book with others, offering them a taste of what God can do when we surrender our dreams over to Him and open our hearts to what He has planned.

—Lisa Copen, founder of Rest Ministries, Inc.,
Author: *Refresh Me, Lord: Prayer for Those with Illness* and
Beyond Casseroles: 505 Ways to Encourage a Chronically Ill Friend
Designer of inspirational jewelry, *Gutsy Goodness*
San Diego, California

ACKNOWLEDGMENTS

Heartfelt appreciation to those who are listed below:

Lisa Copen
Your vision for Rest Ministries begun in 1997 has come to fruition and continues to grow! Hundreds of thousands of those living with chronic health issues, and needing Christian connections with others who understand these challenges, are now enriched in the deepest of ways—His ways. Bless you. I am privileged to call you friend and be a part of your team of devotional writers. This book would never have come to be without your influence in my life.

Mary Lou Koch
How could we have known when we met in 1968 that your one statement to me in 2008, "I think you should write devotionals for Rest Ministries," would evolve into this book? In 1968-69, you helped me teach forty-five first graders how to read at St. Michael's in Silver Spring, Maryland. Now there may be some among them who will be blessed as they read this book! Your friendship, encouragement, and the strength of your prayers has kept me believing during the stand-still times of this journey.

My Fellow Devotional Writers at Rest Ministries
You keep encouragement flowing in my life, along with our thousands of readers who comment about how their lives have been enriched. Your courage facing your own challenges, your support and ceaseless prayers through various crises, and above all your friendships, are soaked in every word that flowed into this book. I pray I represent "us" well. Each of you is evidence that God holds the whole world in his hands. As we have shared in depth from various parts of the United States of America and internationally, we have also come to know how deeply He holds our hearts.

Tim Hansel
Your influence in my life came years before I had the privilege of meeting you. That meeting, which included your wife, Anastasia, brought me two treasured friendships. Your writings helped me take the first steps in learning to live in a body that took an unexpected turn. You helped me discover how God asks and equips us to live out the lives we are given when challenged beyond our ability to believe it is possible. This may not be the book we had hoped to co-write. God called you home before that dream came to be. But I felt you perched on my shoulder as each word flowed forth to become this one!

James Walker

You told me you wanted no acknowledgment when my book was published. I told you that was "too bad" for how could I not give thanks for our years of friendship correspondence, your belief in me, and in my writing. You helped me hone my writing skills because yours were so keen from thirty years as a newspaper journalist for the *Vancouver Sun* in Vancouver, B.C. There was no chance for us to say, "Goodbye," in 2009. As you peek from heaven above, I am here to tell you, "Look what has finally happened, dear James!"

David Severance, Jr.

You are a gift (as well as a dear twin brother) and so was your surprise birthday gift of my first digital camera in 2009 "so I could get really good photos for my book." Thank you for the early editing of some of them before I learned how to do that myself, and for sharing many articles you found about publishing as you encouraged me to persevere and keep my hopes for publication alive.

Apple Retail Store Personnel, Alderwood Mall, Lynnwood, Washington

You have had one enthusiastic student since I bought my first laptop computer in 2008. All I have come to know in using it, I owe to your personable, patient, and expert trainers. I'll look at a photo I learned to edit, a graphic visual design I made, or the Powerpoint presentation I created and see the faces of the ones who were my teachers. You truly are "geniuses."

Dick Staub

Thank you for founding The Kindlings, a relational movement seeking to rekindle the spiritual, intellectual, and artistic legacy of Christians in culture. Although The Kindlings endeavors occur in various venues, it was my attendance in 2010 at KindlingsFest, held on Orcas Island in the San Juan Islands of Washington that put me on the road leading to the publication of this book.

Jerry Root

There you sat at KindlingsFest, 2010, surrounded by your "entourage" at a lunch table. I knew not one soul that first day. Close to stumbling as I tried to find somewhere to sit, you beckoned me to join your group. We exchanged names and then your subtle question, "What's with the cane?" led us into a spirited conversation lasting way past dessert. At that time, having never read one word I ever wrote, you referred me to your friend and literary agent, Stan Guthrie. You, your kindnesses then, and your support ever since, are so appreciated.

Stan Guthrie

Jerry Root paved my road to meeting you. You have graced my life ever since with counsel and consistent encouragement. When doors opened and then closed, you steadied me to keep persevering. During the stretches of quiet inaction, when God was working behind the scenes, your belief in me and my writing remained steadfast. It all has led to his perfect timing for this book's publication. Having your calm reassurances are blessings I will carry always.

My "Sisters in Scripture," St. Thomas More Catholic Church, Lynnwood, Washington

You came into my life at a juncture when much of my mobility and functioning had been leveled. I found you after some months of steps that equipped me to even be at a church. My involvements thereafter with Bible studies have been ongoing, as has your care and inspiration. You are not only sisters, but friends who enrich my life. I love you!

Brookview Community Church, Brier, Washington

Jason Huguenin, pastor (and former first-grade student of mine), I remain amazed at how we reconnected after thirty-four years! Now I learn from you as I listen to you teach. I feel like a "proud mama." And to my Brookview weekly Life Group: your passion as Christ followers, your prayers for me during times I cannot attend, the sharing of our joys, needs, hopes, dreams, or simply taking some evenings to have fun, bring cheer to my world. Each of you is so appreciated!

Photos

I want to thank Dave Peterson and his daughter-in-law, Mary Peterson, for their watercolor images specifically created to image the messages in the texts they accompany. Your artistic talents add a glow to this book's essence. Abundant thanks to each individual who gave me a "personal property release" to use a photo of mine taken on your premises. To the best of my knowledge, at the time of this book's publication, the credits listed are current and may help readers find out more about you!

Friends and Family Members

I am thankful for your prayers and encouragement during my years of hopes and continued endeavors. Each one of you holds a special place in my heart. I am forever grateful for your support in a wide variety of ways.

Redemption Press

Athena Dean Holtz, Publisher: At the helm, you have been gracious in welcoming me and knowing the exact direction to take me and my manuscript. **Amber Payne, Senior Project Manager:** Your warmth, patience, and clarity of function helped me understand and traverse new territory. **Inger Logelin, Senior Editor:** What a dream it was to work with you, step-by-stepping through my texts with your impeccable skills sharpening them in ways that help them shine. **Brittany Torres, Graphic Designer:** Thank you for your expertise bringing my front cover design and interior graphics to perfection, and conveying their theme in your beautifully designed book spine and back cover. And to all with whom I had no direct contact, your part in bringing the project to completion is equally appreciated.

My Holy Three—Father, Son, and Holy Spirit

You beckoned and I said, "Yes," and entered your triune dance. How patiently you guide the choreographed steps you choose for my life. Even when I stumble, your faithfulness holds me steady. You are Life, Love, and Light. I wrap all mentioned above, and the others who take time to read this book, within your embrace as we step in time to the music you have yet to introduce. Amen.

Lynn L. Severance
Lynnwood, Washington
April 2016

DEDICATION

To Tim Hansel, mentor, friend, servant of the Lord, exhibitor of grace, joy, and steadfastness; exuberant encourager to me and countless others during his years of chronic pain and challenges.

At the core of spiritual writing is hungering for wholeness, for self, for meaning. The question, "Who am I?" reverberates quietly in these pages, as does a willingness to be known. I wonder sometimes why I choose to make my spiritual musings visible. I want to believe it is mostly because such vulnerability creates what we might call "a soulful being together" between the reader and the author. A kind of communion born through the meeting of vulnerability and identification. It is in this delicate communion that books bestow their small transformations.

—Sue Monk Kidd, *Firstlight*

INTRODUCTION

Is it possible, during our times of crises and challenges, to know comfort? It is possible, but first it takes a seeking and the understanding that seeking and finding takes time. When we are weary from the drain of life's burdens, there is only one true rest that beckons us to its comfort. We are to seek the One who has said He can give us rest. We allow him to define what we need.

Our Creator has recorded each of our days and knows us thoroughly. He sent a Comforter—his Holy Spirit—who dwells within us and within each challenge we encounter. We can choose to reach for the light of his Presence and encouragement. Many people live with chronic pain, illnesses, or conditions, and never feel the cessation of what these challenges bring to them. Allowing God to help bring the light of acceptance in the face of these circumstances is a type of healing.

When we, and others, are in shorter seasons of trials, choosing to seek direction and comfort from God's indwelling Spirit will move us through these times. There is no way around them. Their realities have to be faced. The worldly momentary comforts will not satisfy for the duration. Dwelling in the daze of crises for too long and refusing the light of hope will move us into deep despair.

In the devotionals that comprise this book, I have chronicled my journey to the conclusions that I have just shared. They did not come quickly. I continue to have struggles as I learn. Ultimately, the lessons have meant positioning myself during times of need to be intentionally seeking and receptive of God's grace. It has meant asking hard questions. "What do you want to do through this challenge and loss in my life, Lord? How can you work through this pain?" It has meant living in the questions and waiting on his responses. I have come to experience God's steadfastness. The ways He has chosen to respond reflect how my faith has grown into light—the light of some of his revelations.

These devotionals were originally written and published online via Rest Ministries. This online Christian-support site has a variety of resources to encourage those living in chronic pain and/or with chronic illnesses. Among its resources are daily devotionals posted on the site and also available via subscription and download to e-readers.

I have revised my writings with the hope that now they will also bring encouragement to those who are going through briefer seasons of trials. The photos I have taken are visual images of each text's messages.

I invite you to join me in this journey. We will learn what can come as we seek the ultimate Comforter's ways of bringing us rest in the midst of our challenges. There are times life's light has dimmed because of how we feel. God may appear to be dim as well. Together we can renew our hope and walk into the Light of his consistent presence, care, and faithfulness.

SECTION ONE

HOPE—FAITH—REDEMPTION—LOVE—PRAISE

I am looking at calendar pages that tell me it is winter in my part of the world. I am also gazing at a vase containing a sunshine-splashed display of daffodils in full bloom. A warming trend compelled these flowers to emerge regardless of a calendar's dictate.

Seasons have rotations and serve their purposes. Yet within traditional expectations, variations can arise. When challenges come into each of our lives, we cannot count on consistencies. A time of joy can be interrupted with unexpected news that brings pain. A time fraught with anxiety can rotate into relief as we breathe sighs of gratitude.

God will work within the challenges of our days. For some, chronic conditions require an intentional daily assurance that He is always near. For others, a season of challenges may be shorter but just as intense in feeling. All of us need the comfort of hope to persevere. We need the gift of faith to access such hope.

With our trust, God can help us traverse any difficulties we face. His love guides us through whatever concerns surface, the ones we never expected on any calendar of our lives.

The writings in this section of the book deal with harsh realities, but the qualities of springtime dominate in their messages. These are gifts God wants to bring to us if we can open our hearts to receive them. Our faith, giving reception to them, is what we return to the Giver.

Bless you as you read!
Lynn

1. Travel Accessories

You have not given me into the hands of the enemy but have set my feet in a spacious place.
(Psalm 31:8)

Am I spending my life in spacious places? My view can seem confining as others rush by me to involvements in many places. Does activity always mean that productivity follows? It seems that as I commit each day to the Lord, He is the one who defines what is productive for me.

I believe strongly that, as Christians, each of us is traveling on the same road, gifted with various talents, yet wearing different shoes. God determines the kind of footwear He hands us for use at various times of our journey. We decide whether to accept or reject our shoes.

They come laced with his grace for the job at hand. They come soled with his promise to travel with us as He knows the way He has ordained we should go. Others' footwear may look more chic but, in his eyes, we can be right in step with what He wants.

God loves and cherishes each of us. He sees us as equal in his eyes and longs that we view one another in the same way. We are stepping out in style with our perfect travel Companion!

There are days we may need sprinting shoes. At other times we could be handed hiking boots for the heavy terrain and for endurance on difficult trails. Perhaps He chooses a pair of dancer's shoes for moments of unexpected joy. After we have experienced a hard day, cushy socks or slippers may await us. How about the occasions we can go barefoot and rest in green pastures!

All times are productive—worthwhile—if God has called us to them. He gives us what we need during this trip called life. Let's thank him, smile at our fellow travelers in their footwear, and cheer one another onward as we travel together.

Lord, thank you for handing me accessories as you guide my life journey. Your will is my security—your grace is my grip. Your eyes value my efforts as I value others accompanying me. We are quite the fashion parade! Amen.

2. Oh, What a Beautiful Morning!

Arise, shine, for your light has come, and the glory of the LORD rises upon you.
(Isaiah 60:1)

I have always loved this verse. It has a joy that bursts with freshness!

Recently, the Scripture came to me in an e-mail. I was surprised as different feelings arose within me when reading it. What had changed?

With some thought I recognized, with my particular challenges, mornings are the most difficult time of the day for me. My mother's cheery voice calling, "Rise and shine," when I was a child, had me bounding out of bed and racing into the day. Even in my younger adult years, mornings were my time to get much accomplished. I savored the quietness of the day's beginnings

Are mornings a more difficult time for you? This is understandable if insomnia has been an uninvited guest. Even sleeping through the night, getting into the day can be a slow process for many. My good intentions are there. I am grateful for the gift of God's new day. Feeling less than strong, I am grateful for his strength that comes through to help.

I own this truth as I pray with sincerity. *Oh, Lord. I don't really arise and shine. I try but it is such intense work. I am grateful for the day. How can I be grateful for the way I feel? I want to return to loving this Scripture verse. I long to appreciate the mornings enthusiastically as I did in the past.*

I process the words. Light can bring joy. Joy can bring a lightness. It says my light has come. The challenges feel heavy.

My focus needs redirection. God's presence is within me. It is the glory of the Lord that rises upon me each new day. Whatever I can or cannot accomplish, the Lord's glory is still upon me. He will help me manage how I feel. I matter that much to him. He is the quiet in the day's beginnings. I can arise and shine with him and for him.

Lord, thank you for shining upon me and noticing all my efforts. Your consistent faithfulness helps me choose to enter each day. What a privilege this is. Now I recognize the joy. It's you!

3. What Are My Real Needs?

"If I send them home hungry, they will collapse on the way, because some of them have come a long distance." His disciples answered, "But where in this remote place can anyone get enough bread to feed them?" "How many loaves do you have?" Jesus asked. "Seven," they replied.
(Mark 8:3-5)

Jesus' teachings nourished the spirits of those gathered to listen to him. During this event recorded in Mark, their need for food was also met. A miracle occurred as Jesus broke bread, had his disciples distribute the pieces to more than four thousand, and leftovers remained—enough to fill seven baskets!

In kind, God cares about my every need. He knows how undernourished I can become in all areas of my life. As someone who lives alone and with chronic illness, how can I evaluate what I am truly needing as each day dawns?

Are my feelings on edge, and my hopes on hold? Is my spirit in need of some freshening? What is in Jesus' basket for me? Among many gifts, I'll find prayers to be offered, strength from his Word, and encouragement to relax and to cease from striving. Yet, in this account, I see something else. Jesus asks his disciples to distribute the food to the crowds. I am designed for relationship both with him and with others.

Do I isolate myself from nourishment that friends could bring? Can I risk letting others know of my need for them? Am I willing to wait for their *yes* if their lives are busy? Chronic illness does not make me exempt from the desire for human connection. It is most important that I have enough. If I become drained, my own opportunity to bring nourishment to others is weakened.

This Scripture passage reminds me the answer to all I need has its foundation in God. He asks others to contribute as they come alongside me. Together, relationships are formed.

The Lord wants no one to collapse on the way Home from lack of care.

Lord, your basket of provisions holds bread, blessed and broken. Your basket is always full. Help me receive from you and from others the gift of relationship. Thank you that you meet every one of my needs in abundance. Amen.

4. Putting the *New* in New

*See, I am doing a new thing! Now it springs up; do you not perceive it? I
am making a way in the wilderness and streams in the wasteland.*
(Isaiah 43:19)

For years I read this verse waiting for a new thing because a new thing was going to be a really *great* new thing. While I waited, my life moved along. I discovered God is the giver of gifts. These come in different packages and in various ways. I prefer gifts that radiate with joy and freedom. I am not confident I have the eyes to see the suffering and pain that infuses my world, your world, the world, as *gifts*.

As a midlife adult I returned to a place in the Rocky Mountains that had good memories for me from my childhood days onward through my high school years. In unexpected ways, I discovered my body was compromised at the higher elevations in Colorado. Events were enjoyed but through a fog of intense physical disorientation.

There came an afternoon when I sat by a creek reminiscing of carefree days in this particular setting. I watched the water flow, come to a rock in the middle of its path, and flow around it, unhindered. It was a nostalgic time. I brought all the years and experiences of *me* to these moments by the familiar creek. God met me that day with some insights.

He sees all of my days from their beginning until their ending. His bringing each day to me is what is *new*. Sometimes there are joys. Other times obstacles emerge. He flows with his grace and with me, either through them or around them. He is with me. I am not to be waiting for him to arrive. Obstacles are an opportunity for his strength to be manifested. His faithfulness is foremost in my thoughts if I stop and remember He has been with me in the past, continues to dwell with me in the present, and He will lead me into tomorrow.

Lord, thank you. With clearer eyes I look upon all my years. The flow of your living water and your strength that never fails, remains consistent. Help me always carry you and this awareness with me. Amen.

5. Cell Power . . . Can You Hear the Call?

"Do not turn me over to the desire of my foes, for false witnesses rise up against me, spouting malicious accusations. I remain confident of this: I will see the goodness of the Lord in the land of the living."
(Psalm 27:12-13)

Mankind. God's masterpiece. Created in his image. We begin our life as one single cell. Then cell upon cell continue knitting together, forming intricacies unique to each of us.

Though created in God's image, we are born separated from him because of mankind's sin. He longs for reconciliation. That was provided when God's Son, Jesus, willingly became man. Eventually, he took all the sins of mankind upon himself, dying in our place upon a cross, conquering sin, and removing the barrier between the Father and us.

This salvation is open to all. With a heart recognition and acceptance of Christ's completed work, we become a single unit once more united with our Creator.

So how can I look at my life, a life created in God's image, a life reconciled to my loving Creator, when the sacred cells He created are not functioning properly? My body seems not my own. I strive. I pray. I grieve. I seek help. I have an innate desire to persevere.

God sees me as whole in him. He knows the completed plan for my life—one I cannot yet see nor fully understand. He hears my prayer, knows my grief, holds me close and whispers, *Be still and know that I am God. I am the overseer of each cell.*

"Lord, I believe you can intervene and touch the cells of life where your plans for me are deeply embedded. Yet I often feel numb, scared, and weary."

I have the supreme authority, Lynn. My Spirit is neither numb nor unaware of what you are going through. I am able to calm the storm of your concerns. Press into me. Listen. Receive my strength. Let any cells of negativity and concern drain away. I will replace them with touches of acceptance and patience. Co-labor with me. Cell upon cell I designed the blueprint that is you.

Can you hear and trust my call? "Yes, Lord! I do hear and trust your call." Amen.

6. Being Called a Friend

———∿∿∿———

I no longer call you servants, because a servant does not know his master's business. Instead, I have called you friends, for everything that I learned from my Father I have made known to you.
(John 15:15)

Friend. What a powerful word. I can count on my treasured friends to be available and trustworthy, to listen and love, to share deeply and empathize.

Jesus calls me friend and is my friend. Friendship is perfected in him. Thus, I struggle with this following paradox. I long to alleviate the suffering of my friends. I can encourage but I cannot heal them of physical or emotional pain. My perception becomes strained as I think upon Jesus, capable of healing, seemingly allowing suffering to remain.

How do I resolve my thought-filled conflict as I trust my truest friend? I come to this conclusion:

I look at how He lived.

He emptied (veiled) his nature as God to take on the nature of man in flesh (Philippians 2:6). He knew all the temptations I encounter. He modeled best how to resolve them. He cried. He grieved. He laughed. He loved. He was misunderstood. He persevered.

I go to the garden of Gethsemane where the human Jesus pleaded with his Father to spare his sufferings (Matthew 26:39). Taking on mankind's sin was beyond anything he had experienced. He trusted his Father, yet, being human, He anguished. Any of my sufferings pale in comparison.

My lesson in the garden? Surrendering involves my trusting what I cannot understand. Jesus' trustworthiness was never deeper than on the cross. After that surrender came victory and mankind's reconciliation to his eternal home.

Jesus now dwells with his Father in resurrection glory. He did all that was asked. My journey here on earth continues. In time, I will understand all that has been asked of me. The Father will make all things clear. Jesus calls me friend, in part, so I can trust the Father as He did.

Lord, because you surrendered, I can surrender. The difficult moments are significant, even bearable, because you call me your friend. I call you Savior and friend. I choose to trust you. I choose to thank you. Being friends makes all this possible. Amen.

7. How Am I Dressing These Days?

Can any of you by worrying add a single hour to your life? And why do you worry about clothes? See how the flowers of the field grow. They do not labor or spin. Yet I tell you that not even Solomon in all his splendor was dressed like one of these.
(Matthew 6:27-29)

As a little girl I loved to put on my mother's party clothes, jewelry, and high-heeled shoes. Then I'd go parading around the house! As a young woman, dressing for special occasions was fun. During these time frames, the outer image seemed most important. I now am more concerned about how I am dressed internally.

A mental mirror checks my attitudes. Are worries consuming my time? Are fears that my challenges will worsen grabbing at my joy? Am I envious of those whose lives seem easier? If these thoughts were seen externally, would I parade around town for all to see me? No.

Yet God sees these inner musings. In my weaknesses, I can labor and spin and get nowhere with these disquieting thoughts and feelings. His words about the lilies help me to focus.

The flowers receive his sunshine and rain. I see how beautifully they are dressed in his attentiveness toward them. I desire to receive God's exhortation to cease from striving. I know his consistent faithfulness and that he provides for all my needs. I have a choice to receive and be thankful for what he gives. I can dress in the comfort of his care.

God regarded me with joy when I played dress up as a little girl. He could see I longed to be lovely. But as flowers grow, so do young girls. My God has been shaping me into his image. He has asked me to let him do the dressing up so, when fully grown, all of who I am is as He intended. Thus clothed, perhaps others will see his image in me, too.

Lord, growing up is hard even when I am already a grown-up! I choose to accept the finery of your lessons even when they seem unlovely. Help me remember you are leading me toward being dressed in your splendor. Amen.

8. Looking at the Glass, Lightly

For now we see only a reflection as in a mirror; then we shall see face to face. Now I know in part; then I shall know fully, even as I am fully known.
(1 Corinthians 13:12)

As I write, it is my birthday. I am grateful for the gift of my life! More than seven decades ago doctors pronounced I would not survive the delivery room. Today, happier words greet me. A former first-grade student writes, "Miss Severance, thanks for learning me good." I smile at his grammatical joy aimed at me!

Have I *learned good,* Lord? You have blessed my days in many ways. I am filled with gratitude. There have been tremendous challenges, beginning with my fight to live beyond the delivery room. At that time you instilled a love within me to choose life. I don't like the trials but I treasure the ways you help me through them. Realistically, looking from *this side of the glass*, parts are smudged and splintered from the challenges and choices that have comprised my life.

I see these imprints because your light shines through showing them to me. I also acknowledge and view the beautiful moments. I choose to recognize both. I desire to dwell in the buoyancy of your light that lifts me above a world that can clamor, wanting to pull me down. Someday I will understand reasons for many of my life events during these past decades. I am in no rush. Delivery to my eternal home will come and all things will be made clear.

It could be that any *whys* that exist now will be unimportant then. I will abide in the knowing and not in any asking. The *learning good* part is my trusting you while looking at the glass of my life lightly. I want to seek your wholeness in what appears broken. In the midst of any challenges, I am still a reflection of you. I want nothing to dim that image.

Lord, every day I see glimpses of beauty amidst the more marred parts of your created world. Help me recognize your touch, especially in my life events that are hard to understand. Knowing you understand can bring me a peaceful contentment. Amen.

9. Seeking Sanctuary

Splendor and majesty are before him; strength and glory are in his sanctuary.
(Psalm 96:6)

I have lived in the same apartment since 1974. Those who come to visit graciously tell me they feel peaceful when they are in my home. I have many remembrances of joys experienced here. When difficulties have entered my life, my home has remained a sanctuary.

Yet, what defines a *sanctuary*? Some would say it is a holy structure such as a church or a temple. I have just called my home a sanctuary. Do I have to be in a particular place in order to feel the security associated with such shelter? When life and its challenges lift my peacefulness, when concerns get heavy, where do I go? I have come to know I can seek sanctuary deep within, where God dwells. His presence is his promise to be ever near.

This psalm does not say strength is in my sanctuary. It says that strength is in God's sanctuary—part of his very presence. He offers his strength to me. He knows I have very little of my own. I am in awe that He wants to dwell within me. I am so grateful he does.

When I am too weary from the battles that rage, He says, "Come and rest." He lightens my load if I let him. I can choose to persevere and overcome with him. He is the shining holy One who keeps my spirit alive and faith burning brightly. Do I get to this place of peace quickly when disturbances enter my life? Not always, but He patiently waits. He trusts and knows I will.

Psalm 96 expands to proclaim the various praises that are due God from all creation. I join in the choruses and give my thanks.

It is not necessary to seek a man-made sanctuary, although they have their place for respite. My refuge is within where I meet with the One who is in residence and yet a part of me.

Lord, I praise you and delight in your faithful and loving presence within me. Your strength can be my strength. Your light can be my light. Together we can shine as a gracious sanctuary wherever we may be. Amen.

10. Shadows

Whoever dwells in the shelter of the Most High will rest in the shadow of the Almighty.
(Psalm 91:1)

The word *shadow* evokes a variety of feelings. Unexpected shadows can bring delight when I see them cast a beautiful design. Conversely, some can bring alarm with their foreboding forms.

This psalm exhorts me to rest in the shadow of the Almighty. I know I can trust his emanating light to provide shelter if I stay close to him. It can deflect shadows that would attempt to intrude on my life and bring confusion. Therein, he offers safety, comfort, and guidance.

As I pondered this concept of *shadows*, I wondered if faith might be like a shadow. Scripture tells me that faith is, in part, "assurance about what I do not see" (Hebrews 11:1). As I am walking with the Lord, I depend on his light and his sight.

The past lies behind me, covered by the shadow that his light, grace, and forgiveness cast upon it.

I am to live in the *now*, trusting the One in the lead.

My future, vague to me, is clear to him. My faith becomes sight when the Lord chooses to move me into the light of what He already sees.

Both connotations of *shadow* are depicted in Scripture. "Yea, though I walk through the valley of the shadow of death, I will fear no evil; for You *are* with me" (Psalm 23:4a NKJV). "Every good and perfect gift is from above, coming down from the Father of the heavenly lights, who does not change like shifting shadows" (James 1:17).

I'll have times of fear. The challenges that life brings long for restoration. When I step outside God's zone of comfort, I falter. I am reminded of how much the security of his shelter provides. I need but take one step back to where He will envelop me.

Faith. Shadows. Both are gifts from God. Both are places where He dwells and invites me to enter in and share the security of a safe space with him.

Lord, our adventures have been many. Your light sheds meaning when I cannot see clearly. I remain grateful that you are my haven of peace as I choose to remain close to you. Amen.

11. Remaining Hopeful

Show me your ways, Lord, teach me your paths. Guide me in your truth and teach me,
for you are God my Savior, and my hope is in you all day long.
(Psalm 25:4-5)

Hope is a key to staying focused on the Lord. It is one of God's gifts I can lose sight of quickly. It happens in the blink of a thought! I stray away for a time. You each know these types of thoughts: fear I have failed God or others, fear I will not get through a time of grief to feel joy again, fear of what a medical test will show, fear of what the future may hold.

I rob the present of God's peace when I worry.

I cringe, catching myself when these times arise. Yet, if negative thoughts go undetected, they escalate. The feelings that accompany them do as well.

When I snap back from my mental straying, I am humbled. My desire is to discern quickly the side trips that have me stumbling off the path where God can teach me. I want my hope focused on him, not on imagining a future yet to come. Looking back upon my former days, I confidently remember how He has never forsaken me.

Some of my *tomorrows* held harsh news. He faithfully steered me through those rough times. I could not depend on my own strength. He and his strength kept me moving, rebuilding my hope in him. These were his deepest times of teaching me, an answer to this psalm's plea.

Scripture tells us there is faith, hope, and love and the greatest of these is love. My perspective that hope is needed to keep me focused does not diminish love. It is God's love that helps me return to his path when I get drawn away. My remembrances that He is my hope strengthen my faith.

He beckons me to follow this triune pattern by putting all three of his gifts into their proper perspective, centered in him. When they work in tandem, I am able to remain hopeful.

Lord, my deepest longing is that I remain steadfast as I love you, hope in you, follow you, and faithfully trust in you completely. Amen.

12. Singing a Song of Zion

By the rivers of Babylon we sat and wept when we remembered Zion. There on the poplars we hung our harps, for there our captors asked us for songs, our tormentors demanded songs of joy; they said, "Sing us one of the songs of Zion!" How can we sing the songs of the Lord while in a foreign land?
(Psalm 137:1-4)

We can feel catapulted into a foreign land when intense challenges are upon us. They wear us down to the point of exhaustion. The temptation to give into the physical and emotional captors is very real, even though our feelings regarding them need expression.

Messages in the Psalms convey the highs and lows that are a part of life events. They also reflect God's faithfulness at all times. Originally sung, now they can bring comfort during our times of upheaval and pain in whatever form we receive them.

Knowing that down through the ages others have struggled with the same cries may help us feel less alone in facing our experiences.

Then my head will be exalted above the enemies who surround me; at his tabernacle will I sacrifice with shouts of joy; I will sing and make music to the Lord.
(Psalm 27:6)

Praise the Lord with the harp; make music to him on the ten-stringed lyre.
(Psalm 33:2)

My faith and trust in God was present during the years before chronic illness erupted and changed my life. In the crucible of these ensuing years, and within shorter seasons of challenges, He has forged a deeper reality of himself.

He understands. He notices. Rather than hanging up his harp of love and comfort, He is ever ready to soothe my soul and heart. He rejoices over me with singing!

I rest in his calming assurance. If I am to be held captive by anything, let it not be by my afflictions but by the One who dwells with me in the midst of them.

Lord, you have entrusted me with your presence. I could choose to cling to yesterday. I would rather walk forward with you and be nourished by the new songs you have for me. With you as my maestro, I want to excel as I sing! Amen.

13. Stepping Toward Spring

Let us acknowledge the Lord; let us press on to acknowledge him. As surely as the sun rises, he will appear; he will come to us like the winter rains, like the spring rains that water the earth.
(Hosea 6:3)

When the calendar indicates spring's arrival is near, I rejoice! The sunshine will beam off blooming flowers instead of warming the soil awaiting the first signs of their emergence. I am ready for a renewal in my body and in my hopes through a stream of sunshine soaking into my being. There will be smiles on people's faces rather than the frozen looks indicating the endurance of winter's harsher elements.

These thoughts remind me there are seasons in our lives. Challenges invade, be they chronic or short term. It can seem like a long winter. A possible refreshment can appear, promising relief. This could take the form of a medical treatment or improved health. It might be a personal breakthrough, emotionally or spiritually. However it comes, it brings a positive spark and a sense of spring's arrival.

There is a different slant in the following translation:

Let us know; let us press on to know the Lord; his going out is sure as the dawn;
he will come to us as the showers, as the spring rains that water the earth.
(Hosea 6:3 ESV)

This quickens some light within me as I await the balm of spring. I press on to know the Lord and his going forth. *Knowing* people is different than acknowledging them. *Knowing* means I have spent time with them and I experience them in deeper ways.

God longs for me to know him, to see him as the dawn, to press on and refuse to dwell in the gloom of my challenges. He moves forward watering the way that has been dry and dreary. As He leads me through the winter, spring shines just ahead. With my eyes on him I won't miss the glow that will soon be in view.

Lord, thank you that your spring rains can revive my crumpled emotions and parched soul. As you help me press on to know you and follow you, glimpses of the dawn come closer. Spring truly becomes a reason to rejoice! Amen.

14. Saying *Yes* at the Edge of the Unknown

I will strengthen you and help you; I will uphold you with my righteous right hand.
(Isaiah 41:10b)

I had sought refuge in a small memorial chapel during an unexpected drenching rain shower. Very minimal daylight was present inside. Tapered candles, lit and placed in trays of sand, were the first images I could see. Then I saw her in sculpture, bathed in candlelight—Mary holding Jesus in her arms at the foot of the cross.

God had chosen Mary to birth Jesus. An angelic encounter brought this news to her. Anointed words greeted her bewilderment, "Do not be afraid" (Luke 1:30). Humbly, Mary said *yes* in agreement. How could she have deeply known what that *yes* would mean? We now know it was a pivotal moment for all of mankind.

In this sculptured image, I viewed a mother looking at the mutilated dead body of her son. This occurred before a Resurrection Sunday. Mary was human and so was her grief. She may have wondered how much more she could withstand from that *yes* murmured thirty-four years earlier.

Yet each of us can have our beginning moments of saying *yes* and receiving Jesus as our Lord and Savior. Our spiritual womb, once void, fills with his presence. How can any of us know where our *yes* will take us?

Such a commitment places us at the edge of many unknowns. It will mean *yes* to plans bigger than our understanding, *yes* to times of both ease and difficulty, and *yes* in faith to follow a risen Lord in trust, regardless of what occurs along the pathway of our lives. The One we follow assures us there are no unknowns to him. "Do not be afraid."

Mary's years of love and faith were not in vain. Neither are ours. With each *yes* we gain strength. It may seem as weak as a small flickering candle's flame, but accessing God's grace, we continue moving into his wider light. One day we will step into the eternal light of home where there will be no more unknowns.

Lord. *Yes*. As those who have gone before me and who were upheld as they walked in your righteousness, I choose to do the same. Amen.

15. Bearing Faithfulness

Remain in me, as I also remain in you. No branch can bear fruit by itself; it must remain in the vine.
Neither can you bear fruit unless you remain in me.
(John15:4)

Jesus speaks of the need to abide in him, that through him I am nourished, live, and have my being. Though I am created in God's image, the living out of this reality unfolds slowly. Jesus modeled how it is done. My choices let God help me learn how to remain in him.

He died to self, in part, so I can abide in him and bear the fruits of his Spirit: love, joy, peace, patience, kindness, goodness, and faithfulness. It behooves me not to flinch when the vine seems confining. I may not completely understand God's ways, but that He died to self means it is something He asks of me. Too much of *me* and weeds compromise the vine!

He wants me to bear faithfulness in two different ways. First are the pruning times known only to the two of us. He knows what He is doing to help me grow, to keep me clinging close, to correct, but never condemn my attitudes or actions, and to redirect my life for his best—and mine. I will feel birth pangs. If I can remain steady, trusting him, I experience resilience of new growth. By his grace and my stillness, his work can be accomplished.

Secondly, I can bear fruit, or carry faithfulness, to those whom I meet as I share God's love with them or toward them. This is an outgrowth of my personal times with him. When I am in settings that make loving difficult, I can remember it is his love I bear. His unconditional love for me can shine through to others when I have experienced it myself. He gives in abundance in order for me to succeed in all He asks me to do.

Lord, you gave your all for me when you died on the cross reconciling me to the Father. Now, as I abide in you, your love and care flow through me. As I am strengthened, we go forth to share love and care with others because I bear your faithfulness. Amen.

SECTION TWO

COMFORT—GOODNESS—PEACE—KINDNESS
FLEXIBILITY

How can we rest when the concerns of life are bombarding us? Our bodies may seem not our own with our emotions fragile. Our faith may be shaken. The joys that once filled our souls are dulled.

There are times I long for the carefree days when a summer vacation was a given! You remember those times—a respite from studying intensely, meeting the demands of someone else's structure, and hoping to pass our tests with flying colors of victory.

Yet life lessons come to us no matter our age. We cannot deny their presence, their demands, and our desire to receive an A+ and move on. In the midst of these times, God has not gone on vacation. He longs to nourish our bodies, revive our emotions, and give hope that fills our souls with the music of his promises. He can bring us to a faith-filled rest that transcends the kind of rest often offered by the world. The peace may pass our understanding, but that only affirms that He is the source.

In the writings that are sequenced in this section of the book, I pray you will find a summer bouquet of inspiration. May you be reminded that encouragement is near to be gathered. It may come in unexpected ways so it is best we keep alert for its arrival. Rather than being forsaken in the midst of our challenges, God will meet us within them with some touches of sunshine.

Bless you as you read!
Lynn

16. Having the Faith of Abraham

He heals the brokenhearted, and binds up their wounds. He determines the number
of the stars; he gives to all of them their names.
(Psalm 147:3-4)

There are revelations in my heart of wounded and broken places. I feel fractured and fragile. Has God forgotten me, or do I need new eyes to understand these promised words recorded in the Psalms? I desire to be well, pray to be healed, and wonder about God's delays in these areas. My life, once embraced with vigor, is seldom vigorous as I face the brokenness.

I know everyone goes through staggering times when life is not only difficult but overwhelming. I pause from some self-absorption, reminded of the time God showed Abraham the starry skies and told him his descendants would number the countless stars above (Genesis 15:5). Abraham could not comprehend such an immense promise. Yet he believed.

As a spiritual descendent of Abraham, I look heavenward to the stars. What can I learn? God called Abraham his friend. He blessed him while acknowledging him as righteous, not because he always did things right or even understood God's ways.

Perhaps I am looking for strength in my fractures rather than looking to the One who wants my attention.

God asks me, *Are you willing to surrender your ways to believe my ways are best? Can you trust me without comprehending my reasons?* I ponder my response. My *yes* will require my flexibility, allowing God's best to rise to the top filling up my fracture lines with himself. That is a reality I desire.

God has the stars in his universe and the plans for my life under complete control. Abraham learned, after that star-filled night, that God's promises for him came to pass. God's plans for me unfold as my heart-pieces rest into his peace and as new life involvements replace former times. I smile at the stars and believe for the *more* that is yet to come.

Lord, I entrust my life to you. As you honored Abrahams's obedience, please honor mine. I receive the comfort of your faithfulness. Remind me to look heavenward toward you when I falter, steadfast in the midst of your stars and promises. Amen.

17. A Gift of Remembrance

See, I have engraved you on the palms of my hands.
(Isaiah 49:16a)

Since I am engraved on the palms of Jesus' hands, then everything, including his recorded days for me, must be there too. His wounded hands, healed, yet scarred, remind me of his sacrifice and death that enabled this engraving.

My memories, thus engraved, are deeply embedded within me. I love the good memories. What takes courage is facing devastating memories head on. Yet God cannot impart his gift of healing until I acknowledge my need for it.

Chronic illness entered my life when I was a mid-life adult. When I suffered intensive flare-ups of internal vertigo spinning, my mother was the person who would leave her home and come to help me. She would hold my head until the worst was over. Remembering her presence brings cherished memories. The memories needing healing were devastating images of her during her last days and moments. I held her head as she took her last breath and died.

God's healing gift came in personal ways. The journey was slow. He streamed an image of my mother— whole, healed, and with him. He did not let up until I could see this stronger image through the dimmer nightmarish veil of other ones.

Her unexpected death left me weak. An opportunity to travel to England quickly surfaced. I questioned if I was strong enough to go. I felt the courage to attempt the trip when I remembered my mother's caring hands that held my head steady.

Far from home, the steps of healing continued. They were ones that only those who have grieved deeply understand.

Walking a sunlit trail in Cambridge on my last day in England, I became aware of a flighty companion. A butterfly was keeping pace with me! My mother loved butterflies. This one was donned brightly in her favorite colors. Cautiously turning on my camera, I captured the priceless moment.

God sent a butterfly. It was a gift of remembrance that my mother was but a breath away with him and, in many ways, still with me.

Lord, some remembrances are difficult. Thank you for the scars you bore so I can turn to you in deep need and come away graciously renewed. Amen.

18. Heartbeats

You, yourselves are our letter, written on our hearts, known and read by everyone.
(2 Corinthians 3:2)

I have lettered family mementos that span nearly two hundred years. Among these treasures is correspondence between my parents during WW II. Though apart, they were *together* awaiting my birth. Heartbeats of chronicled genealogy add up to my feeling grateful for the gift of life.

But first, I was in the heart of God before creation. He awaited his timing to start my heart's beat and delivery to my earthly home. I came with his personalized blueprint of recorded days including his hopes as to how I would embrace his will to contribute to his world.

I continue to desire moving intertwined with the plans He has knit for me—the joys that uplift my heart and the challenges that try it. He is the wellspring of my heart. He is near as I live my life.

Paul wanted the Corinthians to recognize that when they entered into a relationship with Christ, his Spirit came to dwell within them. Christ's love could then be expressed outwardly. This is true for each of us.

How can God's love be released to be read? I know I need to spend heartfelt time with my God in stillness. Within our relationship I gain strength and direction. He reveals part of my blueprint and helps me to live it out.

Hopefully, the caring time I spend with him propels meaningful time with others. I can be a love letter from him. Each person I encounter is also born from the heart of God. I pray I reflect that to them, be meetings brief or ones of longer duration.

When I falter and do not communicate well, my heart can be moved back into the right rhythm. God encourages me to "be strong and take heart" as I hope in him (Psalm 31:24).

As the beat of life goes on within me and around me, I want to be intentional to choose and seize with my mind, heart, and spirit any opportunity to express love.

Lord, thank you that your Holy Spirit keeps wooing me to stay connected to your heart. Thus focused, may my words and actions be read as a glorious expression of your love. Amen.

19. Let All Creation Sing!

Let everything that has breath praise the Lord. Praise the Lord.
(Psalm 150:6)

When God created his works of creation, He declared everything He made as *very good* (Genesis 1:31). In Psalm 150, every part of God's creation is exhorted to give him praise.

God is immutable, incapable of changing (James 1:17; Hebrews 13:8). He looks upon the good in his creation, yet acknowledges the evil that exists from the ways mankind has marred his work.

In Hannah Hurnard's book, *Hinds' Feet on High Places*, the heroine, Much-Afraid, is on a journey guided by her loving Shepherd. As she travels, God's creation is prominent in the lessons she learns as she encounters flowers, waterfalls, rainbows, mountains, and deserts.

My perspective thrives when I read this book. It handed me strengthening lessons before chronic illness became my constant companion. Now, insights go deeper with each reading, encouraging me to stay focused and strong. One lesson connects to Psalm 150.

Much-Afraid discovers a single small flower in the desert. It is sustained by keeping its face toward the sun and drinking an occasional drip of water coming from a leak in a pipe. The flower's name is *Acceptance-With-Joy*.

Unlike mankind, all other creation dwells contentedly in being. Its existence breathes out its praise. Mankind alone chooses if he will respond. From a worldly perspective, this is often viewed merely through one's accomplishments.

God asks that we be content in him. He looks on each heart's intent. There is a place and a balance for both accomplishments and stillness.

I am not to shy away from tasks He equips me to perform but they do not identify me. He does. I often need renewal in understanding this as there are limitations to what I can now do.

I want to accept with joy each season in my life. My Creator asks that I turn my face upward to be nourished by him. Throughout all seasons, one constant remains for me. *I am his.*

This is my praise and He declared everything He made as *very good*!

Lord, I join in the chorus of your loving creation that praises you with joy! May you delight in the gift of songs that breathe out our thanksgiving. Amen.

20. Let's Go Fly a Kite!

You turned my wailing into dancing; you removed my sackcloth and clothed me with joy, that my heart may sing your praises and not be silent. Lord, my God, I will praise you forever.
(Psalm 30:11-12)

Kites dance in the skies! Some years ago, because of a severe health set back, I felt more like a kite stuck in a tree. No medical help brought resolution. At this despairing time, God brought a friend into my life. It was a friendship renewed after some lapsed years. We shared of dreams, hopes deferred, and God's life-light that is always with us and within us.

Along with his care, my friend gifted me with music. One song, "Kite Song" by Patty Griffin, became a part of our friendship language as we prayed for one another and the deep needs in each of our lives. I carry a prayer in my Bible that he wrote for me. Here is a partial excerpt:

> The prayer kites are flying. As a matter of fact I have presented our Maker with the following petition: *Dear Lord, please turn your divine ears my way for just a moment . . . Thank You, Lord. Amen.* I feel every confidence that our loving Watcher will grant my prayer, Lynn. I'm just going to keep it flying toward heaven until He says (in His own way), "Enough already, you've got it." Love . . .

Such thoughtfulness with words of life, light, and song, pulled me out of isolation. It was joy in the midst of a season of pain. I could have remained stuck. Instead, I began to launch prayer kites to dance in the skies with various prayer needs attached to them. Some petitions have been answered. Others await their time.

God knew my needs then and He knows them now. He knows your needs and is ready to meet them in unexpected ways.

Let's go fly some kites! We will attach prayers to soar them into God's loving presence. Once entrusted to him, we will await his perfect timing to respond.

Lord, there is a time for everything under heaven (Ecclesiastes 3). Thank you that in my season of great need, a true friend came bringing hope, love, and new ways to sing and pray. Amen.

21. Love Letters in the Sand

You show that you are a letter from Christ, the result of our ministry, written not with ink but with the
Spirit of the living God, not on tablets of stone but on tablets of human hearts.
(2 Corinthians 3:3)

The day was cold and blustery. I drove the freeway holding tight to the steering wheel to keep my car steady. I began to sing and, surprisingly, the words of the familiar song about "writing love letters in the sand" tumbled out.

It led me to think of the love letters that God can deliver, no matter the season. They come from the soft care in his Spirit's heart but are cemented in his tenacity to respond to my needs. I have known times that hardened *letters* needed expression for they were dwarfing my sense of God's love within me.

Decades ago I spent a summertime week at the Oregon coast. The experience of a deep betrayal months before was within me. Pain and anger would ebb and flow. I had prayed, wept, forgiven, and sought counsel. No release. Just exhaustion.

One particular day dawned in this beautiful beach setting. With sunshine on my shoulders, I wrote out all I was feeling in a letter. I then shouted the words into the vastness of God's ocean. Next, I ripped the paper into shreds and nearly pulverized it into the sands at the ocean's edge.

God's love took the words I expressed, the paper bits, and my emotions out to sea. The cool waters washed over my feet. I stood victorious in his healing peace and restoration.

God is faithful and true. My heart of flesh will experience emotions from loss, hurts in relationships, and challenges within my body. My love for God is built upon trust. I can freely express to him any feelings that I have.

In this experience, God washed away written and then spoken words so the hardness in my heart could be softened.

We exchanged *love letters* in the sand.

Lord, you accept all that holds me captive. As your peace flows into spaces now left empty, my heart fills up with a freedom only you can give. And for that I give you thanks. Amen.

22. Emmaus Eyes

Now that same day two of them were going to a village called Emmaus, about seven miles from Jerusalem. They were talking with each other about everything that had happened. As they talked and discussed these things with each other, Jesus himself came up and walked along with them; but they were kept from recognizing him.
(Luke 24:13-16)

How could it be? These two disciples, having been with Jesus throughout his public ministry unto his death on the cross, did not recognize him after He had risen from the dead. It is said they were kept from this discernment. They may, also, have been overwhelmed in their grief-stricken state—preoccupied with unanswered questions.

Yet, Jesus walked beside them.

As they spoke, He shared the meaning of the Scriptures with them. Still, their eyes were not opened to who He was until suppertime that evening. The simple gesture as He broke bread to eat with them, a gesture known to them, brought forth the needed recognition. The One who had been broken for them in all ways, helped them to see with new eyes that He was their risen Lord.

Christ companioned these two disciples on that road to Emmaus.

Daily, He is a companion to me. Yet often I am *blinded* by my challenges or sidetracked when I focus on what I cannot understand. I falter when it comes to turning quickly to the One beside me who has shown me in the past his love and understanding.

I love reading of this Emmaus encounter. It helps me remember Christ's patience when walking beside me during times I have felt overwhelmed. When I regain my focus, I, too, have eyes to recognize anew my risen Lord.

Will He reveal all the answers I seek? No. Yet I have known the peace and comfort in having him near and in recalling Scriptures that encourage me.

Christ endured brokenness so I can now walk with him. This reality truly gets my eyes opened. All else can fall into place, in his appointed time, as we walk together on the road that leads home.

Lord, "Open my eyes, that I may see, glimpses of truth Thou hast for me." Amen. (Excerpt from a hymn written by Clara H. Scott, "Open My Eyes, That I May See.")

23. Power Sources

You are worthy, our Lord and God, to receive glory and honor and power, for you created all things,
and by your will they were created and have their being.
(Revelation 4:11)

I was experiencing difficulty with my computer. It was not functioning well and would shut down intermittently. An evaluation determined that its battery was not recognizing its power source. This particular problem was repaired, but the incident caused me to ponder my life sources.

My battery, the cells that God created that comprise *me*, were designed to help me function consistently. They regenerate, fostering maximum health. When some cells encounter attacks from within, healthy cells are prepared to come to my body's defense. They assist the weakened ones and help in my body's restoration. There are diseases that can hamper this functioning—but most often this is the design. Truly, "I am fearfully and wonderfully made" (Psalm 139:14).

My spiritual life also has its cells that must be nourished or they will wane. Jesus' Spirit is the power source keeping my spiritual health functioning. He readily comes to my defense whenever I feel weakened. This connection is one of his promises. I am the one who chooses to remain close to him. I need these spiritual cells continually charged with his life.

He desires that all parts of me remain refreshed.

As Jesus needed time apart from busyness, so do I. Conversing with him in prayerfulness, letting him guide me to fresh insights, being still when my body and soul tire, are some of the ways He helps. Ceasing from my own striving allows him to have control.

Peacefulness flows to me through various elements of God's creation: breathing fresh air, rejoicing in a sunset, or holding a loved one. Renewal can replace weariness as I read or listen to a good book. Closing my eyes and allowing beautiful music to fill my soul is one favored way I relax into him.

As I remain connected to his powerful presence, I am prepared to be in fellowship with others, as well.

Lord, in formal and less formal ways you and your power are ever near to restore my weary being. Help me recognize you throughout my day and rejoice in your nearness. Amen.

24. Radiance

Those who look to him are radiant; their faces are never covered with shame.
(Psalm 34:5)

Sunshine is streaming through my windows and it is beautiful. The temperatures will be in a nice range for a comfortable day. I bask in the warmth on days like this. I store up that warmth for the colder days ahead when clouds cool the sun's rays.

I am reminded there is a consistent intangible source of light and warmth available to me. It is not dependent on forces outside of me or weakened by challenges within me. The warmth and light of the Son of God comes with the indwelling presence of his Spirit.

His presence with me, and within me, can be quiet comfort and strength to help as I experience each day. I want to remember to consciously look to him, recognizing He is continuously regarding me with his unconditional love. Just as the sun streams through my window, soaking deeply into my being, that is how He is present. From this depth within, He oversees every moment of my days.

"Those who look to him are radiant." I believe we become radiant when we spend time with our God. He is abundance itself longing to fill us up.

On some of my most challenging days, when struggling seems to be overwhelming me, a friend can say, "Oh, you look wonderful. You must be feeling good." At such times, I know it is God's radiance shining forth. I could choose to go into a litany of my woes, but why?

Why would I change the focus to the negative?

As real as the battles can be, it is more uplifting to realize the source of the glow and to let God shine in spite of how I am feeling. It is humbling as such encouraging remarks make me aware of the Spirit's strength sustaining me.

I say, "Thank you," for God's life-giving and hope-filled light is helping me persevere and beam forth his radiance wherever I may be.

Lord, you look upon me with your perfect radiance. Help me mirror back joy as I accept the gift of you. When my feelings of joy are distant, I rest in the joy of your nearness. Amen.

25. Serving the Lord with Gladness

Make a joyful noise to the Lord, all the earth! Serve the Lord with gladness!
Come into his presence with singing!
(Psalm 100:1-2 ESV)

As I read this verse, I recall early August of 1987 when I was diagnosed with an aggressive form of breast cancer. I was emotionally numb, awakening from surgery to this startling news. The following day, after a sleepless night, a stirring turned me to a flicker deep within. I whispered, "Lord, help me. My eyes are upon you."

I had a deep encounter with the Lord, who came gently with his still small voice. He had to reveal to me what I was feeling. Each emotion was addressed and counsel given. I later realized that He had personally taken me through the first part of Scripture's 2 Chronicles 20. Therein, Jehoshaphat and the people of Judah are awaiting enemy armies that totally outnumber them. Feeling powerless, they turn to the Lord for help.

He tells them not to be afraid:

"For the battle is not yours, but God's . . . You will not have to fight this battle . . . stand firm and see the deliverance the Lord will give you . . . Go out to face them tomorrow, and the Lord will be with you."
(2 Chronicles 20:15, 17)

I relaxed knowing I could confidently face my overwhelming enemy.

The rest of that Scripture has Jehoshaphat instructing his people to go forth to meet the armies, singing praises to God. This became my stance during my months of chemotherapy treatments.

The people of Judah and I experienced victory over a beaten foe.

As to the above psalm's verses? I came to recognize more deeply that I serve a faithful God. He continues to uphold me as I face challenges, some lasting years beyond the cancer diagnosis and triumph. He reminds me very often that the enemy is beaten. I am not.

He is worthy to be served and praised. He first served me as Savior. Now I serve him with a spirit of joy, gladness, and song because He has shown me that is how one celebrates knowing the Lord is the One securing the victories.

Lord, help me continue to make a joyful noise, praising you. Your faithfulness is known, received, cherished, and everlasting. Amen.

26. Well Done, Faithful Servant

Therefore encourage one another and build each other up, just as in fact you are doing.
(1 Thessalonians 5:11)

Today, I received word that a dear friend had died. When I met her in 1971, the first words out of her mouth were, "I'd encourage you to . . . " She became my boss soon thereafter as I worked in an area of the educational field unfamiliar to me. Her words helped me take a risk and step outside my feelings of insecurity. The risk changed my life in positive ways on many levels.

June endured pain and suffering during her last two years of life. When I visited her some weeks before her death, her sparkling blue eyes shone Jesus' love. And, yes, she was still encouraging me!

What is there about words of encouragement that can change my discouragement to hope in an instant? It may not be a physical change, but more of an uplift in my spirit. It is a true appreciation that someone has taken the time to speak affirming support. God knows the right people to place in my life to mirror his love in this manner.

It is a choice to step out of oneself and to think of another person. People who are prone to dwell in negativity will find it difficult. Becoming efficient in positivity may take practice, but it is important and a goal that God's Word tells us to attain (Hebrews 10:24-25).

For June, giving encouragement came naturally. She was content with God and with others. These qualities were contagious. She caught the attention of a widower—intrigued that a sixty-year-old woman could be content and single, having never married. He wanted to know more! At age 63, June married for the first time in 1987. She and this wonderful widower, Charlie, were an inspiration to all who came to know them.

The quality of encouragement that June exemplified remains a part of who I am today. I carry our years of friendship within me always.

Lord, thank you for those who let your light shine through them and exemplify both courage and encouragement. I am inspired to follow more closely in your footsteps as I see how they have paved the way. Amen.

27. Ultra Sounds

The Lord your God is with you, the Mighty Warrior who saves. He will take great delight in you; in his love he will no longer rebuke you, but will rejoice over you with singing.
(Zephaniah 3:17)

God consistently ministers to me through music. It can come via classic hymns, current praise songs, or secular music with spiritual meaning arising from its lyrics. Understandably, this Zephaniah verse is a favorite of mine. Here is how other translations present its end-point message.

"Who will sing joyfully because of you (NABRE).
He will rest in his love, he will joy over thee with singing (KJV).
With his love, he will calm all your fears (NLT)."

As a lover of words, I find the lyrics in a song can reach the deepest parts of me. I have known difficult times when I endeavored in prayer with no evident relief. Then I would hear or remember a song and the needed encouragement emerged.

These verses state that God sings joyfully because of me. Imagine that! He wants to calm me. He is content just to be with me—a quiet calm, soft as a feather sheltered under peace-filled wings.

During the days I was preparing this writing, a medical test required an ultrasound for further evaluation. The test itself was not unnerving to me, but anxiety arose as to what might be wrong.

Listening to music the morning I prepared to leave my home for the appointment, I heard a *perfect* song. I carried it within me. Could this be God's song during the long test?

Medical ultrasounds penetrate deeply into a physical body, discovering details undetected otherwise. For some reason the vestibular dysfunction condition I live with escalated to fearful heights during this test.

Could I feel God or hear him singing over me? No. Did I keep singing internally? Yes.
Did his care penetrate deeply as the medical equipment did its work? Yes.

Was it a duet? It surely was!

Lord, I am aware that the ultra sound I need most to hear is the whisper of your presence in the midst of my turmoil. Thank you that your songs of delight are not dependent on my feelings. Your love and faithfulness is resonating at all times. Amen.

28. Come Away and Rest

I would hurry to my place of shelter, far from the tempest and storm.
(Psalm 55:8)

We are often exhorted in Scripture to cast our cares on the Lord. These are times He can comfort and sustain us. Thus, it is a given such times will come into each life. Nonetheless, they can catch us unawares. Psalm 55 is filled with the cries of one who is distraught and needing the comfort of a calm shelter.

Jesus, our human Savior, needed respite from the crowds and the demands that could drain him. At such times, He stepped apart to be alone with his Father. He did so for direction and relationship, solace, restoration, and peace.

If Jesus needed this kind of rest, how much more will we need the same? Physical and emotional challenges do intensify weariness. We must set aside time to be renewed with the energy of encouragement so we can choose to persevere.

How do you seek restoration during overwhelming times? Are you someone who can get away from your home and discover rest in this way? I have experienced times of refreshment in God's magnificent creation. I love the quiet natural environments where his beauty is manifested. In the quiet, they can *speak volumes* to my soul.

Are you homebound? When I recall times I could be away from home, these remembrances bring joy. The memories remain fresh within me. God blessed me with the events in the first place. He was with me when they occurred and dwells with me in their recollection.

The truth is, wherever we are, God is near and ready for our attention to be focused solely on him. In choosing to spend time with him, any place becomes a resting place. We need but stop and let God meet us where we are.

He is my rest and He is your rest. May each of us allow him to reveal his nearness and care. He loves us and knows what will restore us in the best of ways.

Lord, help me turn my attention to you, recognizing you are my place of refuge. You are ever ready to shelter and strengthen me. And I am ever appreciative receiving your graciousness! Amen.

29. Angel Notes

See, I am sending an angel ahead of you to guard you along the way
and to bring you to the place I have prepared.
(Exodus 23:20)

I learned about God from my maternal grandmother and my mother. I have early recollections of prayer times with them. One prayer focused on a guardian angel appointed by God to be at my side daily. Eventually, I came to hear about other angels, the fallen ones who seek to destroy. The more exciting news was of God's own angels used as his messengers.

As I matured, I became aware of God's deeper presence within me, giving his counsel. His Word indicates He uses both means to guard and guide me.

All evidence points to honor being due God's angels. He used them, not only to give his directives, but to announce life-changing events. Chief among them was a visitation to Mary. With her positive response to an angel's message, God became incarnate within her womb. In time, angels' songs filled the night air heralding Jesus' birth.

Scripture tells us we can be blessed by the presence of God's angels. "For he will command his angels concerning you to guard you in all ways" (Psalm 91:11).

This begs these questions. Are we also messengers of God? Are we called upon to guard those we love, even to help those with whom we are in casual contact? I would say, *yes*. A timely word or an act of kindness can encourage someone who may be struggling. It may possibly bring them safely to a place of hope. Often we are messengers of inspiration in ways we may never know. Likewise, each of us has known *angels* among us whose kindnesses have been very timely, helpful, and inspirational.

Angel notes are all around. We may find them in Scripture, in music, in others' promptings to bless us, and in our guidance to minister life-giving love to them. The hosannas of heaven will be transposed to earth if we are willing to listen, respond, and sing along!

Lord, I ponder the ways your love is manifested to me. Your angels of old inspire me. Angels today bring your care. These notes of blessings singingly cascade and settle deeply within my heart. Amen.

30. Seeking God in the Darkness

One thing I ask from the Lord, this only do I seek: that I may dwell in the house of the Lord all the days of my life, to gaze on the beauty of the Lord and to seek him in his temple.
(Psalm 27:4)

Some decades ago, I was awakened in the middle of the night experiencing the deepest of fears. I reached for my Bible and felt led to read Psalm 27. The following notations are in my Bible from that night. *Let light dispel the darkness.*

Those words kept repeating themselves internally as I read. I was not in literal darkness as I read, but something dark had brought fear and God and his Word lifted it off.

When I have faced circumstances arousing fear, I find myself returning to Psalm 27. Parts of the verse above amplify my appreciation of it: ". . . that I may dwell in the house of the Lord all the days of my life . . . to seek him in his temple."

If I am to seek the Lord in his temple so his light can dispel the darkness, how is this accomplished? As a Christian, I know God's Holy Spirit dwells within me. I choose to seek him in the temple of my spirit's heart. When life is shattering and fearful, my refuge is with him and He is within me.

All the days of my earthly life mean *now*. Whenever any challenge comes, if I choose to seek the Lord, then together we will dwell in his life and in his light.

There are other phrases of inspiration in Psalm 27 that are helpful for those times when fear wells up and attempts to overcome us.

The Lord is my light . . . the stronghold of my life. (v.1)
Though an army besiege me . . . even then will I be confident. (v. 3)
I will see the goodness of the Lord in the land of the living. (v.13)

I acknowledge the light of God within me when I read, speak, hear, and believe these words.

Lord, when I feel overwhelmed and in the dark, I choose to seek you deep within. Together we dwell in the light of your confidence, goodness, and promise to remain forever near. Amen.

SECTION THREE

GRATITUDE—TRUST—FAITHFULNESS
ABUNDANCE—SURRENDER

The leaves are brilliantly colored, maximized in their finery. A nip in the air indicates another season is upon our land. In all this beauty there are notes of surrender. The brilliance will soon lead to a cycle of life as leaves fall to the ground. In time, new growth will emerge from their nourishment.

The leaves' surrender seems so effortless. They yield their abundance willingly. Oh that I could do likewise when needed. I often hesitate, not wanting to let go to make way for the unknown. Yet God consistently desires to give new life. The author of wonder makes *all* things new! He asks my patience as trusting leads to the gift of his faithfulness.

There is an ache in each surrender. When I attempt to do it alone, I can whirl around like the falling leaves. When I seek to partner with my God, He can gently help me fall into his place of grace—a soft landing.

In the writings that fill this section of the book, I have chronicled some of the surrendering steps God has asked of me. It is in the understanding of their importance that my journey with him has moved along. He wants to lead and care for me. He can bring me to a place of trust-filled peace. With a heart of gratitude, He can hear me say, "Thank you, Lord. I am seeing you more clearly now."

Bless you as you read!
Lynn

31. Abundance

Faithfulness springs forth from the earth, and righteousness looks down from heaven.
(Psalm 85:11)

I read this verse and I see eternity and time meeting. I see the seasons of our earth and the need for them. I see God smiling upon me and my returning my best to him. I see what is ideal, even though our earth, and all that is happening upon it, and my life circumstances, may be far from the ideal.

I am reminded that, although created from dust, I am also infused with the breath of God. Besides my creation in God's image is my acceptance of his Son's redemptive death on the cross and his triumphal resurrection. All these gifts culminate with the indwelling of his promised Holy Spirit.

Abundantly full of God!

Could there be more abundance than this? When I read Psalm 85:10, these reflections emerge. "Love and faithfulness meet together; righteousness and peace kiss each other."

How do I recognize the abundance that is within me? Challenges that arise can cloud my view. How do I spring up with faithfulness and flourish right where God asks me to live each day? Such actions seem beyond my capabilities.

The answer lies in my asking a different question. Am I to depend on my feelings or am I to depend on what I know is true? God created me in his image with delicate care. Daily He woos me to reach for him. It is not a reach high into the heavens, but a reach deep within where his Spirit dwells. That is where his abundance rests. That is where I get filled.

We meet. We hold fast to each other as a day progresses. The faithfulness I need is continuing to trust God while receiving the directions He gives. He asks that I keep my focus on him, doing the best I can. We will walk through seasons, some difficult and others less so, but always together.

Lord, as one made from earth and blessed with the abundance of all you are and give, I yield my life to you. As the earth bears its harvest in season, help me to bear the harvest of my days as they remain ordained by you. Amen.

32. Am I Learning, Lord?

Whatever you have learned or received or heard from me, or seen in me—put it into practice.
And the God of peace will be with you.
(Philippians 4:9)

Do not be anxious. Present your requests to God. These are but two exhortations that Paul gives to us in Philippians 4.

Chronic. Ceaseless. These are but two words representing conditions that are plodding and fatiguing. I read what Scripture records and I long to obey. My emotions join in tandem with these longings as I walk a road marked with challenges. If I work too hard at getting every little thing right, I am in danger of an exhaustion that invites failure to be a companion on my journey.

I believe in thinking upon what is noble, right, pure, and lovely. Can attaining such goals become a reality in my daily life? How do I find a balance within myself so I can accomplish what God has asked of me?

Paul learned from what he experienced. He was never healed of his chronic pain. He persevered through many trials besides the thorn in his flesh. He overcame. He learned to be content.

Learned. Practiced. He practiced and learned. He kept his focus not on his circumstances but on God and on what he was led to do. In part, this is what I learn from Paul. My life challenges may be numerous and difficult. What must be ceaseless is my steadfast attention to what God is teaching me. Paul recorded this important lesson. "I can do all this through him [Christ] who gives me strength" (Philippians 4:13).

I want to keep my eyes and heart alert so God can help me recognize the noble and true things. I want to hold onto him and them with integrity. *Practice makes perfect* is no guarantee I will do this perfectly. Keeping my focus on the One who is leading me will help my journey be what He has perfectly designed.

The God of peace is with me. He shines. I follow him, shadowing his peace. Learning. Steadfast. Gradually letting contentment ease on in.

Lord, I have far to go and much to learn. Teach me as you guide me to learn your lessons well. Amen.

33. Confined or Content?

I, the Lord, have called you in righteousness; I will take hold of your hand. I will keep you and will make you to be a covenant for the people and a light for the Gentiles, to open the eyes that are blind, to free captives from prison and to release from the dungeon those who sit in darkness.
(Isaiah 42:6-7)

Any challenges require adjustments. When vestibular dysfunction threw me into a constant state of dizziness and physical disorientation, it happened in one instant. I was blindsided, as if trapped in a dungeon.

What had happened? Why?

Some suggested my faith was lacking or I would have been healed by praying—or by others praying for me. I wondered if I was holding myself captive. I became exhausted believing I had to come to some definitive answers.

When all my efforts seemed a failure, I discovered a new level of dependence on the Lord. He patiently waited for me to understand that He was the only strength I had as I learned to live differently-abled.

I questioned my God-given vocation to be of encouragement to others. Was it possible to proclaim freedom to others and be credible when I felt confined?

Choose life, Lynn. I am asking you for deeper trust. Surrender. I define your life. Let me.

God has helped me take small steps. I experience him literally work through me in spite of how I feel. As I have died to my own endeavors, I somehow rise with him above my circumstances, despite no physical release from their impact. As confined as I have felt, He has remained the open door to meet all my needs. He has shown me the only captivity that ultimately matters is being held captive by his faithfulness.

It is in his faithfulness, I know contentment.

Are there times of struggle? Constantly. Do I choose to trust God and proclaim his freedom? When hope rises to view in spite of my pain and his strength is manifested through my limitations, yes!

Lord, you gave your life for me. Help me continue to recognize the freedom I have in you. You set this prisoner free so I can stand content in you. Amen.

34. I Am Praying for You

The Lord wraps himself in light as with a garment; he stretches out the heavens like a tent.
(Psalm 104:2)

I appreciate praying for others. I certainly have welcomed prayers said by others on my behalf for many of my needs. Primarily, they pray for physical healing and will ask, "Are you feeling better?" I answer truthfully.

"But I don't understand. Why aren't you better? I pray for you all the time."

Such caring words are wonderful to hear. I quickly reply, "Don't stop praying. Your prayers are being used!"

Their prayers help me to reach for God's strength. They are used to come against the times that would attempt to steal my peace of mind and body—or times that have. They are a type of healing as they are a lifting respite of support.

Numerous kindnesses of encouragement have come to me over these years.

I received a prayer shawl knit by one praying for me with each stitch. Another friend sent me an Israeli blue tallit prayer shawl loomed in Africa. It is said that people cover themselves with this large shawl to make a prayer closet—a quick tent! There are fringes that represent the Jewish laws and the hem of Jesus' robe that the woman in Scripture touched and was healed.

I wrap up in the comfort of both of these shawls.

There is a theme of covering with all of these gifts. Prayer is used to cover my current needs. The love of friends surrounds when isolation becomes heavy. I savor such thoughtfulness. In Isaiah 61:3 we are told to put on the garment of praise instead of the spirit of despair. My gifts are tokens that echo that exhortation. They help me persevere.

God's garment over me is our covenant relationship. His love stretches out as a huge tent including with it the many kind deeds and words bestowed upon me from others. Yes. *I am praying for you.* There is power in those five words that I appreciate receiving.

Lord, you are a light of hope and strength as you send special ones to minister to my needs. Keep all of us covered with and within your faithfulness as we bless and comfort one another. Amen.

35. Equipped for the Journey

Those who go out weeping, carrying seed to sow, will return with songs of joy,
carrying sheaves with them.
(Psalm 126:6)

Reading road maps is difficult for me. I have persevered with them when attempting to reach some destinations. I am appreciative that there are better means now for getting access to directions when I travel.

The spiritual dimensions of my life's journey require me to access directions as well. These have been personally mapped out by God. "All the days ordained for me were written in your book before one of them came to be" (Psalm 139:16b). As I read and interpret his map, there are lessons that He teaches me as we travel.

When my life in Christ began, it was faith-filled. There was anticipation of joys. Then testings arrived. Confusion met me as I felt stranded on the side of the road. Yet God was present with his map; and the map showed that his plans for me are good (Jeremiah 29:11). We rerouted and moved on together.

I have come to recognize that God deposits seeds of grace that help me heed and follow his directions. Yet I have had times, thinking I knew better than He, times when I sought other routes and discovered I was lost. I had to backtrack, repent, and humbly acknowledge that God was right in the first place. With my understanding and his forgiveness, we continued onward.

Grace-seeds need time to saturate good soil. Our stopping to rest, and my deepening trust in the One nourishing my way, has enriched the miles we have taken together. There are times of victory that the Lord and I share. He helps me accept the difficulties along the way—some that stay, others that get resolved. When the revelations break through, I gratefully delight.

Awareness of intricate times in my life has helped me seek a closer intimacy with my perfect guide. He and his love instill within me the confidence that He is taking care of me.

Lord, help me draw close to you when my life gets challenging. You equip me, keep me on track, and bundle up my map's days as we approach our intended destination. Amen.

36. Leftovers

Gather the pieces that are left over. Let nothing be wasted.
(John 6:12b)

What a title!

Perhaps it makes you think of food set aside when enough has been consumed to satisfy one's hunger. Those cutting out fabric often are left with remnant pieces. With some resourcefulness, leftover food can create a new meal. Extra fabric can be stitched into a different creation.

I have known times when I have felt like a *leftover.* I wondered where I belonged. When my body's challenges became too intense for me to continue my teaching career, an early retirement was necessary. My planned involvement to volunteer occasionally at my former work site failed.

My caring colleagues remained part of a world where I no longer belonged. I had gifts within me I wanted to offer in service. My illness seemed to curtail those plans.

In this Scripture passage, Jesus had miraculously fed five thousand people. He did this having only five loaves and two fishes and there were leftovers. He saw the surplus as still useful.

Each of us has God-given gifts of high quality. Within them are provisions to carry out the plans He has for our life. God sees no part of us as useless, no matter how limited we may feel. I had to recognize for myself that, if I held onto the former ways that worked so well for me—seeing them as the only way to use my talents—depression set in.

I had to develop new eyes so I could see the different directions God would take me. He helped me gather up the pieces in my life and discover how He had new uses for them.

I choose to trust that God wastes nothing in my life or in yours. "Seek and you will find; knock and the door will be opened to you" (Luke 11:9b).

Who is more resourceful than the One who created us in his image? As each one of us seeks him, may we be delightfully surprised at how God reveals to us the next steps we are to take—and how!

Lord, thank you for the gifts of new life and new ways. My limitations become surplus in your hands. Refresh, rekindle, and use me anew. Amen.

37. Lead the Way, Lord!

Show me your ways, O Lord, teach me your paths. Guide me in your truth and teach me, for you are
God my Savior, and my hope is in you all day long.
(Psalm 25:4-5)

As a young child I learned to ride a bicycle. First, there came a tricycle with training wheels to help me establish confidence driving this type of vehicle. I felt so grown up the day those training wheels were no longer needed. Then, my solo journey with biking began! There were countless days, expanding into years of joyful recreation. Secure in the driver's seat, off I could go as my destination was clear to me.

Then in one instant, the ability to engage in this beloved activity was gone forever.

Were my cycling days over? Not completely. I am still on a journey. I needed a new set of training wheels for a time. Now I have a custom-designed bicycle. God is doing the pedaling as I choose to ride in tandem with him.

He teaches me, as we travel together, because He compiled a complete book of maps. He shows me the way because He is the Way. Some routes are most challenging. He listens to my questions and concerns. Then He helps me to accept the twists and turns because they are a part of his landscape.

I can trust him because He has charted out the course. He assures me I can be secure in his knowing the directions and the destination.

He is my rest when the ride gets too fatiguing. We can stop and I am refreshed in our fellowship. When I am ready for the next stretch of unknown miles, we get back on our bicycle and continue onward.

Every so often He lets me help with the pedaling but He remains in charge of the steering. As He grasps the handlebars, I hold onto him. With his leading the way I can be at peace, for we have had countless days, expanding into years, on this purposeful trip.

Lord, continue helping me on this life journey that you have designed especially for me. I choose to let you lead even when the ways are mysterious. My confidence and trust remain in you alone. Amen.

38. Trustworthy

I thank Christ Jesus our Lord, who has given me strength, that he considered me trustworthy,
appointing me to his service.
(1 Timothy 1:12)

I required medical tests for new symptoms that concerned both me and my doctor. With the weakening of my physical strength and looming apprehension as to what was wrong, my need for spiritual strength was heightened. I prayed for a diagnosis with a positive outcome.

God led me through extremely difficult tests and I experienced his strength. I was to meet with my doctor two days after the tests to find out their results. I planned to stay in my pajamas and rest during the interim day! But *that* day, the phone rang. My doctor wanted to see me immediately.

Such a scenario can elevate anxiety. Yet, as I hung up the phone, a peace descended upon me unlike any I had experienced for some time. It was God's peace. His strength was manifested in the form of peace. What an amazing feeling especially in the throes of the genuine uncertainties.

Oh, the enemy tried to break through that peaceful shield that God wrapped around me. Even the day was gray and rainy as I drove some distance to get to my appointment. The attempts to alarm me were met with that steady God-given strength. This continued as I waited an hour for my doctor in his exam room, still having no clue of what the brain scan had revealed.

In the quiet, I sensed God within me and his still soft voice.
Thank you for trusting me, Lynn.
"Yes, Lord. I do trust you."
That is what I mean, Lynn. Do you understand that as much as you are trusting me,
I am trusting you to trust me?

It was a deep moment, an awe-filled moment. My trust is something God longs to receive. It bonds us in mutual faithfulness. I love him through trusting him. As I do, He can take my weaknesses and give me his strength.

Lord, thank you for the gift of medical tests and doctors that help me. Thank you for the trust that is the bedrock of our relationship. It is not dependent on what tests disclose, for trusting you helps me to face whatever is to come. Amen.

39. A Peaceful Heart

My God, my God, why have you forsaken me? Why are you so far from saving me,
so far from my cries of anguish?
(Psalm 22:1)

We can recognize our feelings mirrored in the Psalms. None of us will ever suffer the torments that Christ suffered on our behalf. However, we will have times of feeling we have been forsaken by him, and by others. Such emotional pain is unbearable.

In reading this psalm, a memory was triggered within me. I recalled an innocent comment that had stabbed at some deep unmet needs in my soul, mind, and emotions. For days this particular pain would not leave me. It was not so much a feeling that God had forsaken me, rather, I was unable to release the pain. My cries were repetitive and coming from a desolate place. I was so busy calling out to God, that it was not until I stopped to take a breath that He could respond.

As his loving answers came, the emotional pain subsided. Tears of gratefulness streamed down my face.

This psalm continues in verse 24 to express more of Christ's tenderness. "For he has not despised or scorned the suffering of the afflicted one; he has not hidden his face from him but has listened to his cry for help."

In my self-centered maze of pain, it may have appeared that God was hidden from me. The reality is He wanted to speak. I needed to get quiet—able to listen.

Come. Face me heart to Heart. You will be able to hand me your bruised emotions when we are that much closer. Let me take the broken pieces. Let me hold you and transfuse new life and hope from my Heart to your heart. I came for this reason so long ago as I cried out in the pain of forsakenness. Only I know how to truly help you now. Receive my peace-filled Heart.

Lord, I hear your invitation to enter your heart and offer you my pain. Thank you for the agonies that you bore for me. As I let go of the burdens I carry, I receive your gifts of all I need. Amen.

40. The Power of Words

*And in his temple all cry, "Glory!" The Lord gives strength to his
people; the Lord blesses his people with peace.*
(Psalm 29:9b, 11)

It is remarkable how letters can join together to form words.

Initially, most people hear words before they learn to speak, or for some, to sign them. Our world of communication widens as we learn to read and write. We have a lifelong relationship with words.

The Old Testament relates how God's words spoke creation into existence (Genesis 1). The Word of God became flesh and dwelt among men. Some of Christ's words are recorded in Scripture to teach and exhort us. He spoke forgiveness while dying and reconciled us to the Father.

Christ's promised gift of his Spirit who would dwell within us, comes to those who choose to receive him. He longs to be deeply present and a consistent source of guidance and fellowship. He has promised to never leave us or forsake us (Hebrews 13:5). These and other amazing grace-filled words from him deserve responses of gratefulness and praises.

And in his temple all cry, "Glory!"

I want my spoken and written words to enhance relationships and my internal words to bring peace, not anxieties. May I not only read God's words in Scripture, but listen to the quiet voice within me that I have come to know is his. I want to speak honestly to him when burdens of my life are heavy. I want to keep my heart open to receive his words of counsel and comfort. Words spoken in confrontation with another can lead toward resolve and peace. May I gather honest prayer-filled words to thank him for his faithfulness.

I cherish the caring words both spoken and written from others. Reception of them has brought joy and consolation. When alone, I have passages in books that change my attitudes, enhance my understandings, and renew my hopes. I never want to underestimate the power of God's words or the effect of my own.

In many configurations, the power of words is revealed. Hopefully, God's glory is revealed as well.

Lord, in this temple where your faithful Spirit dwells, may the glory and light of affirming words be ever in residence and evident. Amen.

41. Homeowner

I will not enter my house or go to my bed, I will allow no sleep to my eyes or slumber to my eyelids, till
I find a place for the Lord, a dwelling for the Mighty One of Jacob.
(Psalm 132:3-5)

During the years of Jesus' ministry, He was a transient. He went where directed by his Father. He preached to those who gathered. He healed many who were in need. He rested when He could with his disciples, a few close friends, or alone. When a teacher of the Law inquired about following him, Jesus replied, "Foxes have dens and birds have nests, but the Son of Man has no place to lay his head" (Matthew 8:20).

While on earth, Jesus restored the path leading back to my eternal home. Completing his redemptive act, He needed to return to his Father. He promised his disciples to send his Spirit to dwell within them. Thus, they would be empowered to continue sharing his teachings. Each of us can make this life-changing choice to have God's Spirit dwell within us as well.

His Spirit within me transformed a spirit that was void of life into a true home. I want to provide a place for him to rest. He wants me to be at rest. I wonder, sometimes, how He must feel in my fragile, challenged body. Then I remember that any strength I have is fueled by his presence.

He has turned me into a homeowner!

He brings the seeds for our garden that will grow his fruit: love, joy, peace, forbearance, kindness, goodness, faithfulness, gentleness and self-control (Galatians 5:22-23a).

With his help, I can be vigilant to notice anything that will disturb our sacred soil. Thieves are ever ready to break in and rip out the seeds that have taken root and are growing. These weeds of sin, doubt, fear, and self-pity are only a few potential home-wreckers. They need to be thwarted so that the garden thrives.

Blooms appear. Bouquets from our home can then be shared with others.

Lord, thank you that your Spirit has come to make all things new, including me! As we dwell together you make our home a haven—a home, sweet home, indeed. Amen.

42. Fingerprints

So I went down to the potter's house, and I saw him working at the wheel. But the pot he was shaping from the clay was marred in his hands; so the potter formed it into another pot, shaping it as seemed best to him.
(Jeremiah 18:3-4)

In the context of this entire Scripture, the Lord addresses the Israelites' sin-filled ways that are in need of repentance. He is seeking the restoration and unity of his people.

Parts of our lives often need reshaping.

We are created in God's image. The process of transformation into that image is ongoing. Repenting means I become aware of needed life-choice changes. As there are some changes only the Lord can achieve, He asks that I put myself into his capable hands.

The following imagery offers me clues about this process. "The potter's house . . . working at the [his] wheel . . . he was shaping . . . as it seemed best to him." The potter—God—is in control. He is personally attentive. The blueprint of my life is one He designed. He does not want me marred and unable to become all He created me to be.

Like you, I have had dreams and plans for my life. There have been starts and stops, detours and surprises along the way to their fulfillment or my acceptance that they will not be fulfilled. When challenges come, for however long they may last, I feel broken. The brokenness may be for a good reason and for God's purposes.

How can God work within my brokenness? Foremost, I committed my life to him. As shattered as I can feel, his good plans for me remain intact. Do I trust him completely? Am I pliable? Can I soften to be honest and share with him all that concerns me? Am I willing to look and acknowledge where my hands have misshapen my life?

When I choose to surrender my control, I become clay in my Potter's hands. I am ready for him to work. His fingers can mold, refine and restore me *as seems best to him.*

Lord, I want your gentle fingerprints all over my life. Help me willingly surrender to you. Work out your will for me—in your way and in your time. Amen.

43. Taking a Stand

Therefore put on the full armor of God, so that when the day of evil comes, you may be able to stand your ground, and after you have done everything, to stand.
(Ephesians 6:13)

I was drawn to the word *stand* in this verse. I live with vestibular dysfunction and it takes effort to stand, sit up, and remain steady. God helps me *stand* firm in other ways.

I recalled a severe setback with this condition and the time it took regaining functioning ability. I cautiously attempted an outing and prayed I would be okay. It was a day-long women's conference, a type of involvement I had once taken for granted. The aftermath of my attendance had me lying on my couch for many days, exhausted and recovering.

The conference was not evil. The messages were encouraging. Standing and maneuvering through the crowds made for a draining day for me physically.

How much can I attempt, hoping and praying that my body does not turn on me?

How do I *stand my ground* where God has asked me to live? Scripture reminds me that his peace transcends understanding. When I am in pieces and feeling no peace, it does not mean He has withdrawn his peace. When I have wavering doubts, his truth is bigger. He says his shield of faith is present to help me fight the battles. Yet, there *is* exhaustion when the battles are strong. My prayers are often whispers of desperation. Praises are more dutiful than emanating from a joyful place.

But what did I hear at this conference, the one that left me physically weakened for days? I heard women share about their times of adversity and proclaim how God had brought them through to victory. They spoke of faith, not failure. They stood to witness with credibility that there is triumph after trials. Perhaps they had spent time on their *couches* as well, discovering the wisdom that encouraged those of us who had come to listen and to learn.

Lord, standing with you will not mean I am always sure-footed. Standing with you means you are standing with me, holding me steady. And for that I am most assuredly grateful. Amen.

44. The Waiting Time

I wait for the Lord, my whole being waits, and in his word I put my hope. I wait for the Lord more than watchmen wait for the morning, more than the watchmen wait for the morning.
(Psalm 130:5-6)

These verses challenge me. Often I am waiting for the Lord, but I am waiting for him to do what I want. The years stretch on and many of my *wants* remain. Waiting is not an inactive time, although it involves stopping and surrendering my plans, allowing God to work.

I am to wait "more than watchmen wait for the morning." At night watchmen guarded ancient cities from atop fortress walls, alert to any potential havoc from invaders. Other watchmen inside the walls worked to keep the city safe. Morning's light bathed many areas out of darkness, lessening some dangers.

The Lord is a watchman for me. When He says, *Wait*, it is for my own protection. He sees what I cannot see. My waiting times can seem as darkness with no certainty shed on the way ahead. It takes soulful trust as I remain stationary. It is a time to hold tight to the Holy Spirit who can help ward off shadows of discouragement and impatience.

My task in waiting is to place my hope and trust in the Lord and not hurry ahead of him. He watches for the right time to pull me out of the dark and into the morning light of his plans. He knows when I am ready to pursue them. He has prepared the way.

There is also the perspective of time that helps me appreciate the wisdom of the ways God has guided me. This fuller clarity helps me understand how some of my choices could have been the wrong ones. I perceive anew the occasions when God grabbed me out of harm's way because I was not careful in heeding his warning signs. Such protection and his watchful care is worthy of thanks and praise.

Lord, the dawn of tomorrow will come soon enough. I choose to wait, trust, and rest with you in the light of today. Help me remember that all of my days are safely in your loving hands. Amen.

45. Planting and Harvest

But the seed on good soil stands for those with a noble and good heart,
who hear the word, retain it, and by persevering produce a crop.
(Luke 8:15)

How do any of us become the fertile soil where the seeds of God's word and life remain rooted? Once it was a given in a garden, but now we must tend to our lives as we journey back home. Thus, if the soil is to become fertile, it will happen along the way.

We co-labor with God, the sower, making choices that lead us toward the harvest of his intent. Some people and experiences impact our lives enhancing growth, while others can rob us of needed nurture depending on our responses.

The seeds of my Christian life were planted by my grandmother, mother, and by teachings at school and church. With a deeper understanding in my young adult years, I made an intentional commitment to Christ as my Savior. Healing from past brokenness was tended to and its tools stored away for future needs. The harvest—*enriched soil.*

I was directed to a career in teaching. God planted within me what was needed as I contributed to the lives of young people. He had graciously nurtured what could have remained barren as a result of my own childhood experiences. The harvest—*joy.*

Yet thorns can invade good soil. One thorn came to me as a virus in 1983. That physical damage remains unrestored. Such blight could destroy God's intended crop. Yet He has helped me dig deeper into the soil, discovering his stronger roots, the ones that hold me close to him. The harvest—*his faithfulness.*

Does this mean I never hurt or get discouraged and weary waging battles to maintain what God intended? No. But deep within I recognize I am more than my illness, my trials, and my failures. By God's grace, I choose to stay rooted in him. He challenges me during desolate times and cultivates the soil. In doing this, He helps me seek and find, persevere and grow. Come harvest time—*a bumper crop.*

Lord, help me stay the course. Keep sowing the seeds that will help me remain rooted and secure in, and with, you. Amen.

SECTION FOUR

COURAGE—PERSEVERANCE—STRENGTH
COMPASSION—INCARNATION

There is no way around the reality of the weather report. I see the snow falling—see the difficulties drivers are having as they try to get to their destinations. Children are thrilled! They joyfully grab their sleds and race to the hills. For others, such wintry times can try our patience as lives and routines get disrupted.

There are seasons when we are asked to endure with a stronger intent. Be it icy roads or deeper life challenges, the temptation may arise to become frigid in our fervor to trust God during what appears an impossible time.

Has He run out of the gifts that were more evident when sunshine filled our earth and our lives? No. His desire is to ever bring us his comfort. Harsher elements swirl bringing their distractions. Instead of slipping off the road, we can dig deeper within, retaining our trust in the One who has the help that we need. We draw on his faithfulness to us in the past seasons of our lives.

We grow stronger in the winter times though feeling weaker. God can manifest his strength in new ways as He holds us close. His love and understanding are consistent, not seasonal. Our love and commitment help us endure what we cannot understand. Rather than fear the slopes at such times, may we cling more closely and let God steer our sled smoothly through to the destination He has planned.

Bless you as you read!
Lynn

46. A Touch of Summer in Winter

But thanks be to God, who always leads us as captives in Christ's triumphal procession and uses us to spread the aroma of the knowledge of him everywhere.
(2 Corinthians 2:14)

It was early December, a month when the fragrances of sugars and spices, and fresh pine boughs may waft throughout homes. Our thoughts turn to celebrating seasonal joys. Should life also present some challenges, a shift in our perspective could bring us to new awarenesses.

Such a time greeted me one December. I was grateful when some insights emerged as I went on a *solo* procession.

I was experiencing side effects from a new medication. Dizziness and imbalance were intensified. The week before my outing, the same effects had eased out. I prayed that same scenario would repeat itself.

As our weather was mild, I chose to go outside and take a walk. My faith and my cane accompanied me. God led the way.

The route I took brought me to a charming house with a white picket fence bordering it. During the summer, hollyhocks and sweet peas abound. The hollyhocks had been cut back, but not the sweet peas. Withered flowers drooped down the wire frame that had supported them when they were in their glory season.

I noticed three sweet pea blooms remained suspended but upright on their vine. Although the sweet peas' literal scent and colors had faded, their form and tenacity remained as if in full freshness.

I felt the Lord whispering encouragement to me. My efforts to hang on had not gone unnoticed. He appreciated my using his strength walking out challenging steps in faith. He saw me clinging to him as my Vine, desiring to flourish when harsh touches in my body could have caused me to choose otherwise.

Those persistent sweet peas must have drunk deeply of the nourishment their vine gave them during sunshine filled days. Likewise, as I cling to God, He offers nurture as I live in the garden of his consistent love and care.

Lord, help me persevere when weariness can overwhelm me. Lead me to the fragrance that is you. Help me breathe deeply, inhaling trust, hope, and the steadfastness that will bring nourishment throughout all seasons. Amen.

47. As We Journey Toward Bethlehem

Then the Lord God formed a man from the dust of the earth and breathed into his nostrils the breath of life and the man became a living being.
(Genesis 2:7)

Bethlehem!

This word, when referencing the city in Palestine—a short distance from Jerusalem—has deep meaning for Christians as the celebration of Christ's birth marks our calendars. His birth is cause for joy during any season, but Christmas time brings forth a focus of more intentionality.

Many festivities commemorate the event. There will be gift giving, card sending, and love abounding as people get together. Music may fill homes as it brings messages of the season to our hearts.

Birth. Wonder. Hope. Fulfillment.

One song that settles deep within me is "Breath of Heaven (Mary's Song)" by Chris Eaton and Amy Grant. The lyrics convey Mary's thoughts on her journey toward Bethlehem and as she struggles with the weight of the imminent birth of the Child she is carrying. Heavy, too, is the responsibility she foresees in raising him.

Mary senses the need for the breath of heaven to hold her together and be forever near her. As she surrenders to God's plan, she recognizes the grace she needs for each of the days to come has also been entrusted to her.

The same weights that overcame Mary can be echoed in the lives of any of us who are living with a chronic condition or working through the trauma of a life event. "Can I bear this burden for one more day? Can I see the gift in this pain entrusted to me? Can I overcome the grief and fears that loom up large engulfing me?"

God's breath of life created us. We carry the breath of heaven within us. His life sustains us. We do not journey alone.

As we ponder Christ's birth, we can commit to a renewal in allowing him to *rebirth* us. We are as dependent upon him as He once was dependent on Mary. We also share in the grace-filled promise that He is forever near.

Lord, I exhale my heavy burdens, making room for you and for your help within me this day. Fill me to overflowing with both the strength and the lightness of your presence. Amen.

48. Let Light Dispel the Darkness

An angel of the Lord appeared to them, and the glory of the Lord
shone around then, and they were terrified.
(Luke 2:9)

Imagine that special night. Sheep were sedate from a full day of following their shepherds and ready for rest, as were the shepherds. The night was clear except for a brilliant star. All was still.

Then—a burst of light, angels speaking, glory outshining that brilliant star—and the shepherds were terrified. Some translations record that they were *sore afraid.* That is mighty scared. That is scared to one's innermost being. It is a huge surge of fear!

A few verses later Luke records, "Glory to God in the highest heaven, and on earth peace to those on whom his favor rests" (Luke 2:14).

Why was this unexpected honor given to the shepherds? Their work was not a job of high profile. They lived solitary lives caring for their flocks. Yet God saw their faithfulness and chose to honor them. His favor rested upon them.

How can these thoughts be of help to us when the unexpected happens in our lives? We feel far from favored, often solitary, and set apart. We tire before day's end. We expect too much of ourselves, often sensing we have disappointed our Shepherd.

Yet He knows each one of us. He knows the longings of our hearts and the times we are *sore afraid.* He knows something else. Light, his light, always dispels the darkness.

How long did the shepherds stay terrified? Once the message being heralded became real to them, they rushed off to Bethlehem. They found the Messiah, a babe in swaddling clothes. Then they proclaimed to all who would listen the wonders of what they had seen and heard.

The stars in heaven continue to sing the same glory. The favor of our Shepherd rests upon us. We can spread his good news to those we encounter during our hardest moments because God's light dispels the darkness. It did long ago and gratefully, it still does today.

Lord, in unexpected places, open my eyes to behold your glories. In whatever ways you choose, help me rush to a Bethlehem near me, proclaiming as I go the wonders you have displayed. Amen.

49. Looking Straight Ahead

For you have been my refuge, a strong tower against the foe.
(Psalm 61:3)

We have all been *there* at some point in our life. Physical symptoms arise requiring medical attention. I found myself roaming in such a stretch of time with God by my side.

Many prayers were being said to uphold me. Investigation was important, although multiple scans and tests made the unknown more intense. A day came when I sat in a specialist's exam room, *oncologist* inscribed on his office door.

God had seen me through a battle with cancer years before this time. That did not make the potential thoughts of a new round any easier. Emotionally, a seesaw existed within me. I would experience peace, but then anxiety would intrude with its *what ifs*. I prayed. "Lord, you made me human and you know what is going on. You are with me and understand my anxiety. You know my heart is trusting you."

My eyes scanned the mid-sized room, an exam table its main feature. A photo graced one wall and an anatomy poster was on another. There was a counter, some magazines, a sink and cabinets taking up the third side. A window filled a large portion of the wall directly across the room from where I sat. I appreciated the natural light offsetting the fluorescent lighting that has draining effects on my body.

I was in somewhat of a daze. Then, I really looked straight ahead. Outside the window, framed within it, the top of another building appeared in full view. It was obviously equal in height to the fourteenth floor room where I was sitting. My first thought was, *That is a strong tower*!

God quickly got my attention showing me an image of how I was to look at him, not at my uncertainties, but directly at him.

I received a good report from the doctor that day. Had the news been different, God's towering strength would have been there as well, holding me steady.

Lord, you remind me not to look behind, or to the left or right, but to look straight ahead, walking confidently with you into my future. Help me recognize you are my strength at all times. Amen.

50. I've Wondered as I've Wandered

Be strong and courageous. Do not be afraid or terrified because of them, for the Lord your God goes with you; he will never leave you nor forsake you.
(Deuteronomy 31:6)

Moments that change our lives dramatically remain embedded within us. When those moments involve health issues or deep losses, we come to view God differently because we need him in new ways. We are in times of confusion and mystery. Our journey to his strength may be equally dramatic.

He will wait for our arrival.

Below I have listed a few events from my life. Perhaps they mirror some of your own experiences. Physical and emotional aspects intertwine when deep changes occur.

A doctor gives a diagnosis of cancer. An accident leaves neurological imprints. Some abilities and functioning are impaired. Independence is forfeited to varying degrees. A beloved career needs to be relinquished. Dreams once pursued are put on a shelf or abandoned completely. Personal faith is questioned by some who believe God heals all those who ask him for healing. There is a degree of abandonment by long-time friends.

In isolation, God remains the constant.

Emotions overwhelm when loss occurs. There are times I have wandered in my thoughts, too bewildered to define what I was feeling. Conversely, I have known feelings ranging the spectrum from numbness, to intense panic, to peace. Looking back, these slow-motion journeys led to resolve. A light deep within beckoned me to recognize I was wondering so I could wander to the only presence I needed. God allowed me time to seek him. Then, with him, I began to learn the steps of our new life.

The steps each of us walks out after great losses will be tailor-made and ordained by God. We certainly wonder and there will be times of daze-filled wandering. If we can stay close to the One who knows where He wants to lead us, we will discover his strength to persevere with renewed purpose.

Lord, when I feel lost, you are continually wooing me to be found by you. Help me recognize and respond to your presence. As you draw me closer and deeper, I will find the strength and direction I need. Amen.

51. Is the Wilderness Always Barren?

A voice of one calling: "In the wilderness prepare a way for the Lord;
make straight in the desert a highway for our God."
(Isaiah 40:3)

Waiting is difficult. Are we to view these times as completely barren? They stretch into months, even years. Such time spans can become overwhelming. God asks for our continuing trust.

Some mentors in Scripture offer us encouragement and hope.

A few months prior to Jesus' birth, his cousin John was born to Zechariah and Elizabeth. This faithful couple were in awe witnessing God's miracle for Elizabeth was long past her child-bearing years (Luke 1).

And what of their son, John? As a grown man, he was long in the wilderness, set apart, and being prepared to minister in proclaiming the coming of the Messiah (Mark 1:1-3).

Jesus, our Savior, spent thirty years in preparation before his public ministry began. Immediately following its commencement, He was led by the Holy Spirit and tested for forty days in the desert (Matthew 4:1-11). Afterwards, He moved forth fulfilling his earthly destiny.

Each lived his life one day at a time. None was idle while waiting on a promise yet to be fulfilled. They engaged themselves in a life that strengthened a personal relationship with God who was guiding them to their next steps. They served where they were and in the acceptance of where they were. They learned to listen to God for his directions.

We see the outcome of their faithfulness. As we struggle with delays, we can look back to our past waiting times that led to an endpoint. We were unable to see then where our days were headed. In retrospect, we may understand how God, in his wisdom, led us to either open or closed doors.

With a change in mindset, we celebrate the gift of each day. We can do all that is asked of us today, knowing that we are moving into God's appointed future.

Lord, you ask me to walk, not in a barren place, but in a deep place with you. Our entire journey is important. Help me appreciate you as the One knowing where we are going! Any wilderness time becomes a place where my trust in you can bloom. Amen.

52. Our Caring Shepherd

As a shepherd looks after his scattered flock when he is with them, so will I look after my sheep.
I will rescue them from all the places where they were scattered on a day of clouds and darkness.
(Ezekiel 34:12)

Scripture is full of caring images of Jesus as a shepherd. Psalm 23 breathes its calming message of our being led beside still waters to receive soul restoration. Luke 15 portrays a shepherd seeking out one of his lambs gone astray and of the rejoicing when it is found.

Though often linked with the principle of salvation, this parable can be applied to any of the Lord's own who have found themselves in unwanted pastures.

The Lord has countless followers who depend on him to meet their needs. In this way, because there are many, they are scattered covering the whole earth. If some choose to wander off, they will never wander from his watchful eyes.

New thoughts emerged in my reading of this Ezekiel verse. I meditated on the challenges that many of us face when we are in relationship with our Shepherd, trusting him and clinging to him for our strength.

Those who do their best to remain close can be crushed by the devastations of life circumstances. This crushing comes on days when clouds and darkness send these sheep into unimaginable dwelling places, often ones not of their choosing. Did the Shepherd make some mistake? No.

What I recognize in this verse is that rescue is not from our wandering off, nor that we are in need of salvation. Rather, we are in specific need of being released from the feelings of despair, guilt, and false condemnation that have overcome us. These bring shadows that threaten to block out the sun of the Shepherd's care.

Yet, He is *closer than close,* embracing each of us. He understands the deepest woundings. He woos us, aware of our need to be nearer to him. We can heal through the receptive touch of the help only He can give.

Lord, I melt into the closeness of your pasture of care. Help me receive the light of your ever-present love. Shine. Destroy any cloud that has taken up the spaciousness that only you should fill. Amen.

53. Do I See His Light Within the Night?

If I say, "Surely the darkness will hide me and the light become night around me," even the darkness will not be dark to you; the night will shine like the day, for darkness is as light to you.
(Psalm 139:11-12)

The challenge of depression is real whether one experiences it as a chronic illness or it emerges at times for a season. Sadly, a stigma still exists surrounding this affliction—but not to God.

Depression is heavy. Adding the emotions of shame imposed by oneself or others brings further distress. Doctors, medications, and therapists can offer help. An understanding of depression's reality and an acceptance of ourselves in relationship with ourselves during such times is essential.

I do not like this unwelcome guest's intrusion. Dwelling with depression and seeing beyond my circumstances and feelings can be difficult. How can the Holy Spirit help? He wants me to see with his eyes. "I have come into the world as a light, so that no one who believes in me should stay in darkness" (John 12:46).

He leads me to these truths:

Nothing can separate me from his love (Romans 8:31-39).
There is now no condemnation for those who are in Christ Jesus (Romans 8:1).
His Spirit intercedes [for me] in accordance with the will of God (Romans 8:27).

Depression feels dark, cold, and unyielding. As there is no darkness in Christ's indwelling Spirit, how can I yield to his light when I am depressed?

I search out other truths.

Hopeless? His plans for me are hope-filled. He remains steadfast in me and with those plans unimpaired. Helpless? He knows He can trust me to trust him *(*1 Timothy 1:12). His thoughts are precious toward me and a part of his light transcending the darkness (Psalm 72:14).

I feel lost when it is dark.
His light never can be extinguished!

When I choose to focus on his Light, I can trust He is there, no matter how I feel.

Lord, you are always present with me. You could never forsake me. If darkness attempts to prevail, you trump it with your light. With you, I can persevere—desiring to dwell within your light-filled peace. Amen.

54. Living Water

Deep calls to deep in the roar of your waterfalls; all your waves and breakers have swept over me.
(Psalm 42:7)

I heard the loud roar before seeing its source. It stirred memories from decades before. I had been on a white-water rafting trip. The *raft* was an individual rubber-styled kayak.

The three-day route proved a waterway through rapids of various degrees of intensity. Often I heard the rapids before seeing them. One trained guide was responsible for three of the individual kayaks and occupants. Each of us was on our own to paddle and traverse the wild rapids following his visual lead.

I was not prepared physically for these churning times. More than once, the strong guide would paddle back up the rapids to rescue me after I had flown out of my kayak. I was whirling underwater in a silent eerie state of disorientation. I learned to relax and let myself float up to the surface out of the chaos. The guide then literally tossed me back into my kayak where I was secured.

The lessons from that rafting adventure have remained with me throughout these ensuing years. There are days when my state of physical disorientation is high. Living alone, I have but one guide to look to for direction in traversing such swirling times so I can stay the course.

The Lord, who helped me relax under those churning waters decades ago, always beckons me to his calming touch. He brings my body's chaos back to a place of stillness. His help is consistent. I am in safe hands for any upheaval that is or that may come.

But what of that deafening roar I had heard that triggered the memories from that kayak trip? I found its source at the end of a trail where I was walking. I discovered a magnificent waterfall that was exceptional in its majesty and beauty. It seemed contained, even content, in its cascading cadence.

Apparently, it knew that its pathway and destiny led to a clear calm pool at its base.

Lord, thank you for meeting me when life's churning uncertainties arise and surprise me. Help me depend on you to sweep me up into your majestic, yet ever-calming presence. Amen.

55. Being Summoned by God

The Mighty One, God, the Lord, speaks and summons the earth
from the rising of the sun to where it sets.
(Psalm 50:1)

Reading the description of creation in Genesis, I am aware that initially God summoned me from the dust of the ground and breathed the breath of life into me (Genesis 2:7). He created me in his image to give glory back to him. I am equipped to respond in a variety of ways. His giving me free will leaves this life-giving choice in my hands.

I allow other things to summon me. They grab for my attention. I do not mean the important things that need to be tended regarding daily care. For me, it is either busyness or lethargy leading to unrealistic expectations that can throw me out of balance. I desire to be watchful, intentional, and tuned in to what God wants for me and from me.

Jesus sought his Father at the rising of each new day. He was summoned by him so they could commune. With the plans for the day established and their fellowship enriched, Jesus went about fulfilling those plans that had been established.

I may not be called to do great things as the world defines *great*. I want to persevere in partnership with God, grateful for the work He has created that is mine. I get caught up in comparison traps—others being summoned by him for different tasks and my covetousness of what they accomplish.

How subtle it can be. Their specific plans are not the unique plans God has for me. He longs that I focus on how I am being summoned by him—what He is saying to me!

I am not to summon myself. That could steer me off track. As I seek direction from God, He will see to it that I hear. If He is silent, that means I am to rest until all becomes clearer. It is important that I am expectant, willing to listen, and ready to follow through.

Lord, from the rising of the sun to its setting, the daytime and nighttime are yours. I commit myself to listen and respond to your daily call. Then, the entire day becomes ours! Amen.

56. The King and I

Let us then approach God's throne of grace with confidence, so that we may receive mercy and find grace to help us in our time of need.
(Hebrews 4:16)

Visualizing a throne, various images from films or storybooks come to mind. I see an elaborate room where those present are either in awe, or in dread of a king seated before them.

This verse refers to a spiritual throne room where God, the one eternal Being, the King of Kings, has always existed. Within him are three persons (the Trinity), each coequal and coeternal with the other. Though taking on different functions, each remains fully God and becomes known to me because of his role affecting both my natural and eternal life.

Redeemed: The person of God, the Father (Creator) designed the plan to reconcile me (each of us) back unto himself within time and into eternity.

Teamed: The person of God, the Son became flesh (Incarnation). He entered time, teamed with me in humanness, and carried out the Father's redemptive plan. He took on my sins (all mankind's), died and conquered death (resurrection), so I could be reconciled to God.

Seamed: The person of God, the Holy Spirit is the indwelling presence of God, freely sent after the Son of God completed his redemptive act and returned to the Father. He seams up and completes the Trinity's presence in my spirit. The Spirit of truth, proceeding from the Father, testifies about the Son of God (John 15:26). With his grace-filled guidance, I can choose to walk out God's plans for my life.

What a throne room! With the King's compassionate love, gifts abound. I am saved, have an eternal destiny, and am forgiven when I confess my times of failure. There is restoration as I walk through times of questioning and sorrow-filled grief.

Throughout the events in each season of my life, grace flows during times of fellowship in the throne room. Rejoicing arises as there becomes a singleness of purpose and agreement.

"I have given them the glory that you gave me, that they may be one as we are one: I in them and you in me. May they be brought to complete unity . . ." (John 17:22-23a). Amen.

57. Servanthood

In your relationships with one another, have the same mindset as Christ Jesus: Who, being in very nature God, did not consider equality with God something to be used to his own advantage; rather, he made himself nothing by taking on the very nature of a servant, being made in human likeness.
(Philippians 2:5-7)

How often my thoughts and feelings rule my attitude. Like the leaves wind-ruffled or bombarded by a turbulent storm, my attitudes can be all over the place. How do I seek stability?

I can look at Christ's stability. He served his Father, agreeing to enter time and take on man's human nature. By his death and resurrection, He achieved his divine purpose—my reconciliation to the gracious, rightful inheritance as a child of God. I choose to accept the inheritance through belief in what Christ accomplished.

A servant is one who is tireless in his commitment as a devoted follower. For me, this would mean a follower of Christ. He was a servant to all. He perfected servanthood beautifully. He never wavered from the commitment He made to his Father. I learn from Christ's example as I remain committed to him.

I seek to attain attitudes that are Christlike.

He was not immune to life's cruelties. He endured opposition to his teaching. He was deserted by his closest of friends when He needed them the most. He met distress head-on. He was firm, acknowledged reality, and managed to respond in love. When his human efforts tired him, He spent time alone seeking nourishment and direction in prayer.

God asks that I stay steady toward him when the harsh challenges of life assault me. As I turn to him, I remain his servant. Christ knew that a higher purpose would unfold from his obedience. He knew that dying to self is true servanthood.

In my covenant commitment with him, I choose to emulate what He beautifully modeled. He gave his all. He desires I do likewise. He offers me his strength to accomplish this task.

Lord, help me continue to seek a stance of steadiness in my attitudes, becoming more like you. I want to accept and grow in the way of life you modeled when you became the servant of all. Amen.

58. Promises, Promises

May your unfailing love be my comfort, according to your promise to your servant.
(Psalm 119:76)

Each day brings variants to what we may experience. There are times that stun us in what arrives unexpectedly. We cry out for a place to turn for comfort and calm.

This verse is a plea to access God's unfailing love, a promised comfort. For some, their challenges create intentional daily pleas. Others will plead as challenges emerge.

Here are a few of God's promises.

Never will I leave you; never will I forsake you. (Hebrews 13:5b)
For I know the plans I have for you . . . plans to prosper you and not to harm you, plans to give you
hope and a future. (Jeremiah 29:11)

Nowhere among these and other promises from God's Word, does it say *how* He will fulfill them. My life's road may twist and turn causing me to wonder how He is working. I may not sense his presence or have any sense of hope.

My body and heart can become weary.

Yet I know *God is love*—the greatest of his gifts. I know He is faithful. I need but look back to promises fulfilled from my past pleas. They are recorded in my daily journals and are embedded within my heart. They give cause for praises, thanks, and hope in knowing that I can confidently trust him.

"In the morning, Lord, you hear my voice; in the morning I lay my requests before you and wait expectantly" (Psalm 5:3). I desire to be his devoted follower. Even when I falter, He never does. His love never fails nor do his promises.

God is honing my unconditional love for him as He fulfills his promises. He'd rather I focus on this than on my feelings or understanding of *how* He will bring fulfillment. With my trust and faith in him, we share confidently on the road to his revelations. I have made a promise to follow him, no matter the cost.

Indeed, both of us are promise keepers!

Lord, when I become impatient, help me stop and remember my promises to you. Serving you means trusting you—your love, your timing, and your ways. The reality of your faithfulness will keep me strong. Amen.

59. Looking Beyond the Mountain of Affliction

The mountains melt like wax before the Lord, before the Lord of all the earth.
(Psalm 97:5)

In 1983, eight months after the onset of what I came to find out was vestibular dysfunction, friends invited me to a prayer breakfast. The main speaker had a healing ministry. After our meal, he offered to pray with any who had needs.

When my time came for prayer, he laid hands on me—including putting his fingers into my ears. As he sincerely prayed, I experienced the sound and the feel of a rushing wind swoosh through me. I was reminded of Pentecost!

Some were healed that morning. I was not.

The man who prayed encouraged those of us who had not experienced healing to remain hopeful. He compared our need to a huge mountain. God was behind that mountain, chipping away. In his appointed time, what seemed insurmountable to us would cave in.

I have come to realize during these ensuing years, that there are many kinds of healing. I have asked God to help me know what He has been chipping away—what areas in my life have needed his attention.

Where once I depended on my own strength, He has chipped away an over-dependence on self. When I had to leave a beloved teaching career, He reminded me there are different ways to serve him. He has helped me understand that the quality of how I serve him is more important than the quantity of my accomplishments. As some people exited my life, others have entered and become caring friends. Where once I fought my affliction, God has helped me come to an acceptance of what I cannot change. He still bestows many joys.

There is more to learn. I have handed him the tools so He can choose what needs attention. He alone knows the outcome He wants to achieve in all I experience. As I surrender and trust him, He can accomplish his work.

Lord, help me look beyond the afflictions that often pound hard upon and within me. I am in your capable hands. When I cannot see nor understand the tools you are using, thank you for continuing to work behind the scenes on my behalf. Amen.

60. Seasoned

But the land you are crossing the Jordan to take possession of is a land of mountains and valleys that drinks rain from heaven. It is a land the Lord your God cares for; the eyes of the Lord your God are continually on it from the beginning of the year to its end.
(Deuteronomy 11:11-12)

On the first day of each new year, I read this Scripture passage. It is a reminder that another year has arrived. I know it will hold seasons of days.

Before I look forward, I look back on the highlights from the year just completed. Yes, there were mountains and valleys. I came through them! I will face joys and challenges in the year ahead. I intend to walk into the unknowns of each new day aware of God's faithfulness. He guides me if I choose to let him.

True. The Lord cares about the land and the year. But He cares about me more.

His presence is steadfast. His eyes are continually on me. He desires my cooperation as He accompanies me daily with his grace. I best not dwell on each day of the *whole year.* That would be overwhelming! God sees those days ahead. I release them into his caring hands.

I commit to accepting his grace as I live out one day at a time. Will I discover it to be a mountain or a valley day or somewhere in between? Maybe it will be a day comprised of all three!

As I read this Scripture, I know I will have questions as some of my days arrive. That is alright. Seasons from other years in my life have helped me recognize that my *not-knowing* is simply part of God's *all-knowing.* He sees the land's obstacles. I trust and follow his lead. I become a seasoned traveler by choosing to accept both the mountain days and the valley days.

Each nourishes me as I drink the rain from heaven—God's presence itself.

Lord, you are my constant Comforter as I face the seasons of my life and the unknowns of each day. Thank you for being my hope, my trust, and my guide as I treasure you in each of my moments. Amen.

Samplings of Encouragement from Lynn's Bookshelves

The Holy Bible (various translations).
Peterson, Eugene. *The Message.*
Abbott, Winston O. *Sing with the Wind.*
Augustine, Saint. *The Confessions of St. Augustine.*
Brand, Dr. Paul and Philip Yancey. *Fearfully and Wonderfully Made.*
Brand, Dr. Paul and Philip Yancey. *Pain: The Gift Nobody Wants.*
Burnett, Francis Hodgson. *The Secret Garden.*
Bell, Geoffrey T. *God Holds the Key.*
Billheimer, Paul. *Don't Waste Your Sorrows.*
Bonhoeffer, Dietrich. *The Cost of Discipleship.*
Runyon, John. *The Pilgrim's Progress.*
Callahan, Marjorie and Patricia Kelley. *Final Gifts.*
Cameron, Julia. *The Artist's Way.*
Card, Michael. *A Fragile Stone: The Emotional Life of Simon Peter.*
Chambers, Oswald. *My Utmost for His Highest.*
Chapman, Gary. *The Five Love Languages.*
Chittister, Joan. *The Gift of Years: Growing Older Gracefully.*
Claypool, John. *The Light Within You.*
Cloninger, Claire. *Dear Abba: Finding the Father's Heart Through Prayer.*
Cloninger, Claire. *Postcards from Heaven: Courage and Comfort from God's Heart to Yours.*
Cohen, Richard M. *Strong at the Broken Places: Voices of Illness, a Chorus of Hope.*
Copen, Lisa. *Refresh Me, Lord: Prayers for Those with Illness.*
Cowman, L.B. *Streams in the Desert.*

Crabb, Larry. *66 Love Letters: A Conversation with God That Invites You into His Story.*

De Saint-Exupéry, Antoine. *The Little Prince.*

Dunn, Ronald. *Will God Heal Me?: Faith in the Midst of Suffering.*

Edwards, Gene. *The Divine Romance.*

Edwards, Gene. *The Prisoner in the Third Cell.*

Edwards, Gene. *A Tale of Three Kings: A Study in Brokenness.*

Eldredge, John. *The Journey of Desire: Searching for the Life We've Only Dreamed Of.*

Eldridge, John and Brent Curtis. *The Sacred Romance: Drawing Closer to the Heart of God.*

Elliot, Elisabeth, ed. *The Journals of Jim Elliot.*

Foster, Richard J. *Celebrations of Discipline.*

Fox, Mem. *Wilfrid Gordon McDonald Partridge.*

Guyon, Madame. *Union with God.*

Graham, Ruth Bell. *Sitting by My Laughing Fire.*

Grahame, Kenneth. *The Wind in the Willows.*

Guthrie, Stan. *God's Story in 66 Verses: Understand the Entire Bible by Focusing on Just One Verse in Each Book.*

Hammarskjöld, Dag. *Markings.*

Hayford, Jack. *I'll Hold You in Heaven.*

Hayford, Jack. *A New Time and Place: Ruth's Journey of Faith, Preparing Yourself to Receive God's Best.*

Hansel, Tim. *Dancin' Toward the Dawn* (formerly *Through the Wilderness of Loneliness*).

Hansel, Tim. *You've Gotta Keep Dancin'.*

Hendricks, Shelly Benoit. *You're Chronically Ill . . . So Now What?.*

Herring, Annie. *Glimpses: Seeing God in Everyday Life.*

Housden, Roger. *For Lovers of God Everywhere: Poems of the Christian Mystics.*

Houselander, Caryll. *The Reed of God.*

Hurnard, Hannah. *Hinds' Feet on High Places.*

Keating, Thomas. *Open Mind, Open Heart: The Contemplative Dimension of the Gospel.*

Keller, Phillip W. *A Shepherd Looks at Psalm 23.*

Kendall, R.T. *Total Forgiveness.*

Kidd, Sue Monk. *Firstlight.*

Kidd, Sue Monk. *When the Heart Waits: Spiritual Direction for Life's Sacred Questions.*

Klein, Gerda Wissman. *All But My Life.*

Kreeft, Peter. *Back to Virtues.*

Kreeft, Peter. *Making Sense of Suffering.*

Lawrence, Brother. *The Practice of the Presence of God.*

L'Engle, Madeleine and Luci Shaw. *Friends for the Journey.*

L'Engle, Madeleine and Luci Shaw. *Herself.*

Lewis, C.S. *Mere Christianity.*

Lewis, C.S. and Don Giovanni Calabria. *Latin Letters of C.S. Lewis.*

Lewis, C.S. *The Problem of Pain.*

Lewis, C.S. *Till We Have Faces.*

Lindbergh, Anne Morrow. *Gift from the Sea.*

Lindbergh, Reeve. *No More Words: A Journal of My Mother.*

Lotz, Anne Graham. *Why?: Trusting God When You Don't Understand.*

Lucado, Max. *Traveling Light.*

Lucado, Max. *When God Whispers Your Name.*

MacDonald, George. *The Diary of an Old Soul.*
Manning, Brennan. *The Ragamuffin Gospel.*
Marshall, Catherine, ed. *The Prayers of Peter Marshall.*
Marshall, Catherine. *Something More.*
Moberg, Marilyn. *The Zippered Heart.*
Mehl, Ron. *God Works the Night Shift: Acts of Love Your Father Performs Even While You Sleep.*
Mehl, Ron. *The Tender Commandments: Reflections on the Father's Love.*
Miller, Calvin. *The Singer Trilogy.*
Miller, Calvin. *The Table of Inwardness: Nurturing Our Inner Life in Christ.*
Morgan, Robert. *The Red Sea Rules: 10 God-Given Strategies for Difficult Times.*
Norris, Kathleen. *The Cloister Walk.*
Nouwen, Henri. *The Return of the Prodigal Son: A Story of Homecoming.*
Nouwen, Henri. *The Wounded Healer.*
O'Connor, Elizabeth. *The Eighth Day of Creation.*
Palmer, Parker J. *Let Your Life Speak: Listening for the Voice of Vocation.*
Peterson, Eugene. *Leap Over a Wall: Reflections on the Life of David.*
Piper, John. *The Passion of Jesus Christ.*
Piper, John. *A Sweet and Bitter Providence: Sex, Race, and the Sovereignty of God* (based on the book of Ruth*).*
Rilke, Rainer Maria. *Letters to a Young Poet.*
Roberts, Frances J. *Come Away My Beloved.*
Rosenberger, Gracie and Peter W. *Gracie:Standing with Hope.*
Rupp, Joyce. *Praying Our Goodbyes: A Spiritual Companion Through Life's Losses and Sorrows.*
Shaw, Luci. *God in the Dark: Through Grief and Beyond.*
Shaw, Luci, ed. *A Widening Light: Poems of Incarnation.*
Sittser, Jerry. *A Grace Disguised: How the Soul Grows Through Loss.*
Smith, F. Lagard. *Meeting God in Quiet Places: The Cotswold Parables.*
Stepanek, Mattie J.T. *Journey Through Heartsongs.*
Swindoll, Chuck. *Come Before Winter . . . and Share My Hope.*
Swindoll, Chuck. *Growing Strong in the Seasons of Life.*
Swindoll, Luci. *The Alchemy of the Heart: Life's Refining Process to Free Us from Ourselves.*
Tada, Joni Eareckson. *A Place of Healing: Wrestling With the Mysteries of Suffering, Pain, and God's Sovereignty.*
Tada, Joni Eareckson and Steve Estes. *When God Weeps: Why Our Sufferings Matter to the Almighty.*
Wiesel, Elie. *Night.*
Wangerin, Walter Jr. *Mourning Into Dancing.*
Wangerin, Walter Jr. *Preparing for Jesus: Meditations on the Coming of Christ, Advent, Christmas, and the Kingdom.*
White, E.B. *The Trumpet of the Swan.*
Wiederkehr, Macrina. *Seven Sacred Pauses: Living Mindfully Through the Hours of the Day.*
Vanauken, Sheldon. *A Severe Mercy.*
Voscamp, Ann. *One Thousand Gifts.*
Young, Sarah. *Jesus Calling: Enjoying Peace in His Presence.*

Photo Credits

Cover
Sunrise on the Sea of Galilee, Israel (1979)

Section One

Hope—Faith—Redemption—Love—Praise

Introduction—Lynn's Daffodils.
1. Travel Accessories—Poulsbo, Washington (2010).
2. Oh, What a Beautiful Morning!—Sunrise on the Sea of Galilee, Israel (1979).
3. What Are My Real Needs?—Mukilteo, Washington (2009).
4. Putting the *New* in New—Brinnon, Washington (2009).
5. Cell Power . . . Can You Hear the Call?—C.S. Lewis' home, The Kilns, Headington, Oxford, England (2001), http://www.cslewis.org.
6. Being Called a Friend—The Garden of Gethsemane, from a watercolor by Dave Peterson, Edmonds, Washington (2010).
7. How Am I Dressing These Days?—Christianson's Nursery, Mount Vernon, Washington (2010), http://www.christiansonsnursery.com/.
8. Looking at the Glass, Lightly—Molly Ward Gardens, Poulsbo, Washington (2009) http://www.mollywardgardens.com/.
9. Seeking Sanctuary—Jamestown Settlement, Jamestown, Virginia (1990).
10. Shadows—Grantchester, Cambridge, England (2002).
11. Remaining Hopeful—River Cam, Cambridge, England (2002).
12. Singing a Song of Zion—Linda Hill-Phoenix, San Diego, California (2010), music minister and celestial harp therapist.
13. Stepping Toward Spring—Ireland (1979).
14. Saying *Yes* at the Edge of the Unknown—Holyrood Catholic Cemetery, Shoreline, Washington (2010).
15. Bearing Faithfulness—The Heins' home (Finn Hill), Poulsbo, Washington (2010).

Section Two

Comfort—Goodness—Peace—Kindness—Flexibility

Introduction—Molly Ward Gardens, Poulsbo, Washington (2009), http://www.mollywardgardens.com/.

16. Having the Faith of Abraham—"Abraham's Promise," from a watercolor by Dave Peterson, Edmonds, Washington (2010).
17. A Gift of Remembrance—Cambridge, England (2002).
18. Heartbeats—Lynn's home, Lynnwood, Washington (2010).
19. Let All Creation Sing!—Skagit Valley, Mount Vernon, Washington (2010), courtesy of Washington Bulb Co., Inc./RoozenGaarde daffodil fields.
20. Let's Go Fly a Kite!—Seattle, Washington (2009).
21. Love Letters in the Sand—Del Mar Beach, Del Mar, California (2010).
22. Emmaus Eyes—Poulsbo, Washington (2010).
23. Power Sources—International Fountain at Seattle Center, Seattle, Washington (2010), http://www.seattlecenter.com.
24. Radiance—Lynn's neighborhood, Lynnwood, Washington (2009).
25. Serving the Lord with Gladness—Lynn's home, Lynnwood, Washington (2009).
26. Well Done, Faithful Servant—C.S. Lewis' home, The Kilns, Headington, Oxford, England (2001), http://www.cslewis.org.
27. Ultra Sounds—Lynn's home, Lynnwood, Washington (2010).
28. Come Away and Rest—Molly Ward Gardens, Poulsbo, Washington (2009), http://www.mollywardgardens.com/.
29. Angel Notes—Holyrood Catholic Cemetery, Shoreline, Washington (2010).
30. Seeking God in the Darkness—Lynn's home, Lynnwood, Washington (2010).

Section Three

Gratitude—Trust—Faithfulness—Abundance—Surrender

Introduction—"Mountain Majesty," oil painting by Maggie Severance.

31. Abundance—Silver Lake, Everett, Washington (2009).
32. Am I Learning, Lord?—Cambridge, England (2002).
33. Confined or Content—C.S. Lewis' home, The Kilns, Headington, Oxford, England (2001), http://www.cslewis.org.
34. I Am Praying for You—Philadelphia, Pennsylvania (1990).
35. Equipped for the Journey—Seattle, Washington (2010).
36. Leftovers—Hand-stitched quilt by Lynn, Lynnwood, Washington (2011).
37. Lead the Way, Lord—Molly Ward Gardens, Poulsbo, Washington (2009), http://www.mollywardgardens.com/.
38. Trustworthy—Ireland (1979).
39. A Peaceful Heart—St. Thomas More Catholic Church, Lynnwood, Washington (2010).
40. The Power of Words—C.S. Lewis' home, The Kilns, Headington, Oxford, England (2001), decor and artistic design, Nichole Fazio; hostess, Cynthia Smith, http://www.cslewis.org.
41. Homeowner—Grantchester, Cambridge (2002).
42. Fingerprints—Jamie Zach, Kingston, Washington (2011).

43. Taking a Stand—United States Marine Corps War Memorial, Arlington, Virginia (1990). The design of this statue is based on the AP photo by Joe Rosenthal taken during the Battle of Iwo Jima, February, 1945.
44. The Waiting Time—Lynn's neighborhood, Lynnwood, Washington (2010).
45. Planting and Harvest—Stocker Farms, Snohomish, Washington (2010), http://www.stockerfarms.com/.

Section Four

Courage—Perseverance—Strength—Compassion—Incarnation

Introduction—Lynn's neighborhood, Lynnwood, Washington (2009).
46. A Touch of Summer in Winter—Lynn's neighborhood, Lynnwood, Washington (2009).
47. As We Journey Toward Bethlehem—"Bethlehem Journey," from a watercolor by Dave Peterson, Edmonds, Washington (2010).
48. Let Light Dispel the Darkness—"Shepherd Fields," from a watercolor by Dave Peterson, Edmonds, Washington (2010).
49. Looking Straight Ahead—Saint James Cathedral, Seattle, Washington (2015), http://www.stjames-cathedral.org/narthex.aspx.
50. I've Wondered as I've Wandered—Bodega Bay, California (1985).
51. Is the Wilderness Always Barren?—Orcas Island, Washington (2011).
52. Our Caring Shepherd—"An Embracing Rescue," from a watercolor/mixed media by Mary Peterson, Edmonds, Washington (2015), http://funkyfibers.net.
53. Do I See His Light Within the Night?—Via Dolorosa, Jerusalem, Israel (1979).
54. Living Water—Brinnon, Washington (2009).
55. Being Summoned by God—Cambridge, England (2002).
56. The King and I—Lynn's home, Lynnwood, Washington (2010).
57. Servanthood—Cambridge, England (2002).
58. Promises, Promises—Lynn's home, Lynnwood, Washington (2015).
59. Looking Beyond the Mountains of Affliction—Bob MacPherson's home, Lynnwood, Washington (2010).
60. Seasoned—Mt. Baker from Mt. Constitution, Orcas Island, Washington (2010).

Questions for Personal Reflection or Group Discussion

Section One
Hope—Faith—Redemption—Love—Praise

1. **Travel Accessories**
   a. What grace do you need for a challenge currently in your life? If God were to hand you a pair of shoes to walk in during this time, what would they look like?
   b. Think of one person whose life is vastly different from yours. What are the qualities that you value in this person? How does this person inspire you to be your best?
   c. Recall one of the harder times in your life and how God brought you through it. What key points from his encouragement would you use to help someone else facing his or her current challenges?

2. **Oh, What a Beautiful Morning!**
   a. Recall a moment when you were surprised by joy that could only have come from the Lord? How did you know it was him?
   b. Think about this day. For what are you grateful?
   c. Were there parts of this day that brought disappointments? How did God help you face them?

3. **What Are My Real Needs?**
   a. When you awakened this day, what were your first thoughts? Your first feelings? How did these beginnings of the day affect your whole day?
   b. When you find yourself depleted from a lack of connection in relationships, what do you do to remedy it?
   c. As you reached into God's basket of provisions for you this day, what did you find? How were his provisions used?

4. **Putting the *New* in New**
   a. Think about a favorite memory from your early years. What feelings emerge as you recall it? In what ways are the feelings the same or different than when you had the experience?
   b. What is a *new* thing you sense God is doing in your life? What makes it *new*? How has it affected your relationship with him?
   c. How has God's strength been manifested to you during times when obstacles filled the pathway of your life?

5. **Cell Power . . . Can You Hear the Call?**
   a. What stories have been passed along to you regarding your birth? In what ways have you come to know you are a masterpiece from God's hands?
   b. Recall the experience when you knew you were reconciled to God through the redemptive power of Jesus' death on the cross. What feelings emerge as you recall this reality in your life?
   c. What storms in your life have been calmed by God's presence and assurance that the two of you are co-laboring when life gets difficult?

6. **Being Called a Friend**
   a. When you think of your closest friend, how has he/she encouraged you in your times of need? Likewise, in what ways do you bring encouragement to him or her?
   b. What is the deepest surrender you have had to make up to this point in your life? Recalling this surrender, what were the steps needed for you to bring that surrender to completion?
   c. In what ways have you experienced the reality that Jesus has called you his friend?

7. **How Am I Dressing These Days?**
   a. What worries can spiral you downward into negative thinking? What do you do to reverse this process?
   b. What character quality do you possess that needed shaping by God in order for it to bloom and be used for good?
   c. What personal weakness seems to be the hardest for you to overcome? How is God helping you to transform it?

8. **Looking at the Glass, Lightly**
   a. Choose one beautiful moment or event in your life. What makes it memorable? How do you recognize God's touch in it for you personally?
   b. Choose one of the most challenging moments or events in your life. What makes it memorable? How has God helped you recognize that He was with you personally as you faced that challenge?
   c. In what ways can any event in your life, when you allow God's light to shine on it, make a difference in how you view it?

9. **Seeking Sanctuary**
   a. Where do you find the perfect physical environmental place for you when you need sanctuary? In what ways does it bring you nourishment?
   b. When you seek spiritual sanctuary deep within, how would you express the experience you have at these times?
   c. In what ways have you been a sanctuary of comfort for another person who was in need?

10. **Shadows**
    a. When caught in the shadow of fear or uncertainty, how can you respond to the light that is making the shadow visible? How can you respond to the light of God that wants to break through to encourage you?
    2. In what ways has faith helped you keep walking straight ahead out of the fears or disappointments of past days?
    3. As you anticipate your tomorrows, knowing God is aware of what each day holds, how does your faith help you live fully engaged in today?

11. Remaining Hopeful

a.   What is the one thing that can attempt to rob you of hope? What means have you discovered that help you prevent the robbery?

b.   How has God worked with you in past times when your "hope tank" was low on fuel? What means did He use to fill you up again with himself and with his confidence to persevere?

c.   Share some key ways that God has "guided you in truth and taught you."

12. Singing a Song of Zion

a.   Have you ever found yourself in a "foreign land" of confusion, even feeling that God was far away? If so, how did you find your way back to him and to the song in your life?

b.   Has there been a time in your life when God put a new song in your heart? How did it happen and how did you share your song?

c.   Revisit one of your favorite Psalms. How do you find yourself renewed in the visit? What parts of it sing into your heart?

13. Stepping Toward Spring

a.   Can you recall a long winter season of challenges that seemed never ending? What happened that helped you get a glimpse of spring light ahead that filled you with promise?

b.   Are you currently in a long winter season that seems never ending? How do you hang onto hope at such times? What can you do to draw close to the hope that is dim?

c.   The Lord's "going forth is as sure as the dawn." He wants to take us with him. How do you choose to follow him even when you are enduring a time of physical and/or emotional pain?

14. Saying *Yes* At the Edge of the Unknown

a.   What unknowns have you faced, when your *yes* to stay committed to the Lord plunged you into deep grief? How did your heart become restored?

b.   Often in Scripture we are exhorted: "Do not be afraid." Yet fear is an emotion that can easily be kindled. How do you trust this exhortation and still remain true to what you feel?

c.   Recall a time when saying *yes* at the edge of the unknown brought you to a positive direction in your life. In what ways did this increase your faith and trust in the Lord's ways?

15. Bearing Faithfulness

a.   How are you feeling about abiding in God's vine this day? Is it a nourishing time or a time of pruning? What are you doing to bear either one?

b.   What does faithfulness mean to you in your relationship with the Lord, with others, with yourself?

c.   How would you define "dying to self"? What has it meant in your life? How has it changed your life?

Section Two

Comfort—Goodness—Peace—Kindness—Flexibility

16. Having the Faith of Abraham

a. When you recall an overwhelming time in your life, how did God get your attention to turn your eyes toward him?

b. What plan or promise have you had to surrender to God's timing? How has that changed the ways you think about his plan and/or promise?

c. What stars in your "hope chest" did God finally let shine—just for you? How long did you wait for this fulfillment to come into your life? How have you expressed your gratefulness?

17. A Gift of Remembrance

a. In what ways has God helped you to walk through deep grief due to the death of a loved one?

b. What qualities did your loved one leave as a legacy of remembrance for you? How have you integrated those qualities after allowing the initial grief to soften you and bring you strength?

c. Contemplating Christ's nail-scarred hands, look at your own hands. What gifts can you see engraved there because of his work in your life? What are his gifts of remembrance for you?

18. Heartbeats

a. What is uppermost, at this time in the heartbeat of your life? How is God directing you either in joy or in resolve to keep your heart beating with his rhythm?

b. What is the gifting that God uses in you to get *his* heart and *your* heart beating as one? As you are "known and read" by others, what do you convey and how do you best convey it?

c. What do you do when you find your heart out of step with God? How do you recover and revive the life-stride that you need with him?

19. Let All Creation Sing!

a. Pray. Prays. Praise. As you look at this progression of words, what responses come to your mind? What does each word mean to you?

b. What parts of God's creation, outside of mankind, fill you with awe? What attributes touch a deep part of you? How can you incorporate these and make them a thanksgiving for the gift of your life?

c. How can you *sing* during the despairing times in your life? How do you stay connected to God? How do you discover the one drop of his encouragement that will help you persevere?

20. Let's Go Fly a Kite!

a. When have you experienced the encouragement of another lifting you up and out of your distress? How was the view of your circumstances changed knowing he or she understood your heart and your pain?

b. In what ways can you bring joy to a friend who is in the midst of a season of distress?

c. What prayer needs at this time in your life would you attach to the tail of a kite, launch into the skies, and entrust into God's hands?

21. Love Letters in the Sand

a. In what ways do you consider yourself a letter written by the Spirit of the living God? What do you hope others will read when they view your life?

    b. What edits are currently being done in your heart to help you become a blessed reading to others?

    c. How is God speaking to your heart at this time? Are you able to respond? If not, do you know what is holding you back? Write him a letter sharing your feelings, read it aloud to him. Quietly wait for his response to you.

22. Emmaus Eyes

    a. What besetting thoughts can consume you, swerving you off balance as you progress through your day? When you become aware of their pull, how do you regain your balance?

    b. If God were to open any of the Scriptures to your understanding, choose two or three that you would present to him for clarity?

    c. What personal concerns do you currently need to pour out to God as the two of you walk on *your* Emmaus road? How have you recognized his ways of responding to you in the past that could help you to listen now?

23. Power Sources

    a. As you check your physical, mental, emotional, and spiritual batteries at this present time, how would you rate their level of efficiency?

    b. What means have you found that best helps you to recharge any battery within you that needs attention? How can some of the charged batteries come to your assistance?

    c. Knowing that God ultimately provides the means to restore us, how do you respond to the ways He restores you?

24. Radiance

    a. Is radiance dependent on how you feel, or is it available when choosing to receive God's grace? Is it is a feeling, a knowing, or both?

    b. In what ways do you experience the light of God's presence when you are physically or emotionally weakened?

    c. How do you and your life come up shining in spite of your circumstances? Do you have to wait until you feel like it to encourage another?

25. Serving the Lord with Gladness

    a. Recall a time when you had no recourse but to allow God to be strong for you? How did you feel letting go of your control so He could take over?

    b. When obstacles arise, how do you stay secure in serving the Lord? When the obstacles are pain and sickness? When you feel you want to quit serving?

    c. How would you describe the *enemies* that quickly can rob you of your joy in serving the Lord? How do you combat them?

26. Well Done, Faithful Servant

    a. How would you describe someone who consistently encourages you? How are his or her ways of doing this perfectly suited for you?

    b. Has anyone seen through your insecurities noticed potential in you for a new task? How did you respond? If the Lord led you to step out in faith, in what ways did your life change for the better?

    c. How does being encouraged inspire you to be of encouragement to someone else? What are the ways best suited to you that help you convey encouragement to others?

27. Ultra Sounds

    a.   What sounds are the most soothing to you? What is there about them that reaches into you in such a personal way?

    b.   How do you experience God delighting in you? What sounds does He use that are uniquely notable for you? If you do not experience his delight in you, how can you access this promise and make it real for yourself?

    c.   In what ways have you experienced God's faithfulness to you? How might these experiences be the quiet sounds that speak to you of his delight?

28. Come Away and Rest

    a.   What is there in your life at this present time that is the most overwhelming? How are you reacting and/or confronting it?

    b.   What conveys rest and calm to you? A setting, a person, an activity? How often do you allow this restoration to be a part of your day?

    c.   Are there experiences in your past that can bring calm as you revisit them in reflection? How do you allow God to go back with you to those times so that together you are restored in the gift of them?

29. Angel Notes

    a.   "I am sending an angel ahead . . . to guard you." What does this promise from God's Word mean to you? What are your remembrances of a time when you felt divinely led to a new place? What made the experience of this place just right for you?

    b.   Recall when timely messages in any form came to you. In what ways were they delivered?

    c.   When have you felt strongly prompted to be the message bearer (in any form) to someone in need? How did you accomplish this task and how was it received?

30. Seeking God in the Darkness

    a.   Fear can be a rational or an irrational emotion for any of us. How do you respond when either kind of fear strikes? What have you found personally helpful when dealing with this emotion?

    b.   Read through all of Psalm 27. Choose some verses (or individual words) that illuminate your understanding of God's promise to be your strength in times of trouble.

    c.   When are the more prevalent kinds of times you seek God more intentionally? In what ways do you seek him? Do you find him or are you found by him? How does the seeking and restoration help you?

Section Three

Gratitude—Trust—Faithfulness—Abundance—Surrender

31. Abundance

a. How would you define *faithfulness* as it applies to you? To God?

b. Elaborate on the ways you have experienced God's faithfulness. How do you maintain a stance of faithfulness to him?

c. Can you describe how, or if, you recognize the abundance of God that is within you? Is the manifestation tangible or dependent on other means of discernment?

32. Am I Learning, Lord?

a. What lessons are you currently learning? How is God helping you learn them well?

b. As you look back on the years you have known a committed relationship with God, how would you assess the growth you have experienced?

c. What are the noble, right, pure, and lovely things that you can perceive in your life at this time? What diversions could move your attention from them? When focused elsewhere, how do you find God at your center again?

33. Confined or Content

a. In what ways do you experience a covenant relationship with God?

b. How has this covenant helped you trust in him, especially during difficult circumstances?

c. At this moment in your life, do you feel confined or content? Are there ways you can recognize a steadfast freedom no matter your feelings? How?

34. I Am Praying for You

a. There is power in prayer. In what ways would you agree with this statement? Why?

b. Do you have a favored way to pray for others? How are you comforted in knowing you can pray for others? Do you need to know how your prayers are answered for them to be effective?

c. How do you feel knowing Christ is interceding for you in prayer at all times? (Romans 8:34.)

35. Equipped for the Journey

a. What is one significant lesson you have learned in your faith journey with the Lord? How did the lesson evolve? Are you able to maintain the lesson or have you needed refresher courses?

b. What has been your most difficult stretch of miles so far? How did God guide you through them? What could you tell a struggling fellow traveler to make his journey more hopeful?

c. If you are someone with a chronic health issue, or more than one, how have you been equipped to handle this unexpected part of your life?

36. Leftovers

a. Have you found your life redirected in unexpected ways, at unexpected times, making you wonder where you fit? How did you discover there was a new life to be lived?

b. How has God rekindled a gift you have to offer, using it in new and meaningful ways?

c. How could you encourage a friend who is going through an intense life change? What surplus from your life experiences would bring inspiration and hope?

37. Lead the Way, Lord

a. Are you consciously aware of letting the Lord lead you in your life? How did this relationship develop?

b. "I am the way and the truth and the life" (John 14:6a). How do you interpret these words of Jesus, as they relate to the life you are living?

c. Various metaphors convey how the Lord is leading us. Is there a metaphor besides a bicycle that is more suited to you and your journey with him? How did you come to this view?

38. Trustworthy

a. What does it mean to you to *trust God*? How do you trust God?

b. How have you trusted him with an overwhelming occurrence in your life? If that experience has been resolved, what were the key steps in walking it out? If you are still in that experience, how is God helping you?

c. In what ways does your perspective change as you realize how deeply God is trusting you to trust him?

39. A Peaceful Heart

a. When have your experiences robbed your heart of its peace? How did God help you journey to a deeper place with him so emotional healing could take place?

b. Have you ever felt forsaken by God? How were you able to recognize his presence within you again? How would you share with another who is presently feeling forsaken by God?

c. Do you need a spiritual transfusion at this time? How will you hand your brokenness to God so He can work his healing deep within you?

40. The Power of Words

a. What would you choose as the three most meaningful words in your vocabulary? What feelings do they evoke in you? How do you use them in communicating with others?

b. What words would you choose from God's Word—words spoken by Jesus—as the most meaningful to you? Why are these your choices?

c. What have been the most meaningful words written to you personally, ones that enhanced your life?

41. Homeowner

a. As you contemplate being a homeowner with God's Spirit in residence within you, what kind of home do you desire? How would you describe the condition of your home at this present time?

b. What thieves are prone to lurk around your home? What safety locks have you established to ensure they have no access or that they have a quick exit if they ease on inside?

c. Which fruit of the Spirit is a favorite of yours? Why? Which of the fruits do you feel the Spirit needs to tend to in order for it to flourish within you?

42. Fingerprints

a. When has brokenness in your life taken you to the *potter's wheel*? How was God able to reshape the part, or parts, of you that needed the attention of his design?

b. How do you think any of us become pliable so God can do his transforming work? What reality in your life brought this to your personal awareness?

c. God's fingers have molded you. How can you now touch others' lives using the imprint He has made in yours?

43. Taking a Stand

a. Ephesians 6:13-17 speaks to the many pieces of armor we are to put on each day so we can stand firm in a relationship with God. Read these verses and choose one armor piece that is the most meaningful to you. What makes it significant?

b. How do you come against doubts that attempt to rob the peace of God's steady sustaining presence within you?

c. When have you had to take a stand for what you believe as a Christian? What helped you persevere when opposition from others was strong?

44. The Waiting Time

a. In the past, how have you handled waiting on the fulfillment of a need in your life? Did you feel a certainty of the fulfillment or was a total surrender to the Lord's will required?

b. How has God grown patience within you as you have waited on him?

c. Recall a time when unanswered prayers were God's means of protecting you from harm. Recall when you did not heed warnings, but God brought you through in spite of your choices. How have both experiences shaped your view on the importance of waiting on God to unfold his best for your life?

45. Planting and Harvest

a. How do you stay rooted in God so you are the good soil where He can easily deposit the seeds He has for your life?

b. How does God cultivate you and help you remove the rocks and weeds that can put your crops in danger?

c. How would you describe the current season you are experiencing? Is it a planting time? What specific seeds has God sown and how are you tending them? Is it a harvest time? What is in the crop you now can see in its full glory?

Section Four

Courage—Perseverance—Strength—Compassion—Incarnation

46. A Touch of Summer in Winter

a. Winter's harsher elements require a stronger focus. How do you seek the strength to persevere when life challenges become weightier?

b. "Jesus Christ is the same yesterday today and forever" (Hebrews 13:8). With this perspective, how can the constancy of Christ help you face any season?

c. Recall times when your life was tangibly lighter, in full bloom with wellness. God's fragrant enduring love has not changed. What is stored in your heart that will help you reach for him now?

47. As We Journey Toward Bethlehem

a. What life burden weighs heavy upon you this day? What feelings does it bring to you? Is it possible to surrender a burden with an act of the will, while feelings may take longer to resolve? How? In what ways might this perspective lead toward lightness?

b. How might God breathe grace into your life so you know it is a gift from him? How do you open yourself to him?

c. *Lord, hold me together with your heavenly breath.* How might you rest, meditating on this prayer?

48. Let Light Dispel the Darkness

a. Can you recall a time when you were terrified to a point of being immobilized? How long did the intensity last? Moments? Days? Years? Perhaps fear still reigns in you.

b. God is light and He wants to herald it into our fears. How can you seek him in his light when it is hard to feel anything but the dominating fear?

c. Read Matthew 7:7. By faith, rest in a solitary moment with a glimmer of light from God. Can you feel a difference? If it is a positive difference, seek more times like this with him.

49. Looking Straight Ahead

a. When you have times of extreme uncertainty, when a daze of anxiety overwhelms you, what do you do?

b. Do you feel God is surprised by the life events that confront you? What could overtake you (or any of us) that is beyond his grasp or help?

c. Can you discover God's strength by looking straight at him, ready to receive the strength that He wants to give to you? One help could come by reading Psalm 18:28-30 NLT.

50. I've Wondered As I've Wandered

a. When have you known an intense experience that left you unable to access your feelings?

b. There are times when the full expressions of all we are feeling would be unbearable. Can you recall how you moved from numbness in your experience to the beginnings of expressing your feelings? In what ways did God help?

c. In recalling this time, what do you recognize as God being emotionally protective toward you? Read Psalm 139: 7-12 NLT and Isaiah 43:13 NLT.

51. Is the Wilderness Always Barren?

a. What kinds of wilderness times have you experienced in your life? When you were in the experience, could you grasp hold of any hope? If so, how? If not, what did you hang onto?

b. Are there any blooms of insight in your life now that were cultivated *within* you or *for* you while you were set apart in your wilderness experience?

c. How would you express your experience of God or with God while the wilderness time dominated your life?

52. Our Caring Shepherd

a. I was *"scattered on a day of clouds and darkness."* Have you been in unimaginable places, desolate, covered by a mantle of shame? Those times are impossible to forget.

b. What steps did God help you take toward the reception of his healing grace to restoration and wholeness?

c. If you are still under the mantle of your shame, can you consider that God desires to invade the feelings holding you hostage? Would you allow others whom you trust to partner with God and help you take the needed steps? He has offered rescue and security within his embrace. (See Romans 8:38-39 NLT.)

53. Do I See His Light Within the Night?

a. If you experience depression, chronically, or on occasion, describe how it feels to you.

b. What aspects of your experiences do you want to fade under the brightness of God's light? What does it mean to you, knowing He understands all you are feeling?

c. Light and darkness cannot dominate at the same time. How could this help knowing that God and his light are within you to give you a hopeful perspective?

54. Living Water

a. Have you experienced life rapids that threw you whirling out of control? How did you manage to resurface? Were you alone or did you have help in your rescue?

b. If the challenges you're facing could be measured, how deep do they go? How deep is God's love for you in all you encounter? "Reach down from heaven and rescue me; rescue me from deep waters, from the power of my enemies" (Psalm 144:7).

c. Christ calmed storms at sea and calmed those in turmoil. He is living water. Why do you think *water* is mentioned often in connection with Jesus' teachings?

55. Being Summoned by God

a. Jesus was summoned each morning to meet with his Father. He gained strength for his day. In what ways has God summoned you? How did you discern his call? How do you discern it now?

b. In what ways do you get caught comparing yourself to another with a different calling? If so, do you let it deflate your own call or devalue theirs? How?

c. Our lives can be summoned to experience the deepest of challenges. How have you met such times? In what ways has God helped? In what ways have others helped you?

56. The King and I

a. How would you define *grace*? How do you experience it in your life? Can you receive it easily and give it to others graciously? In what ways?

b. As you contemplate the persons of the Holy Trinity, how have their works most deeply influenced your life? Do you find yourself turning in thought and/or prayer to one person (Father, Son, or Holy Spirit) more then the others? If so, why?

c. Read John 17. As Jesus speaks to his Father, sharing how the work He was sent to do on earth was completed, which verse or verses mean the most to you personally?

57. Servanthood

a. Jesus, though equal with God, veiled that equality for a time to accomplish his earthly tasks as God's Son. He modeled for us how to serve. In what ways do you want to emulate Christ's servanthood?

b. If each of us is called to serve one another, how do you experience having another person serve you?

c. When you are deeply challenged, does your definition of *serving* change? How? For those chronically ill, how do you perceive your call to serve when the fatigue and pain are ceaseless?

58. Promises, Promises

a. There are hundreds of promises in Scripture. Choose a few that you turn to for encouragement. In what ways do you experience these promises?

b. How do you view the promises that are foreign to your experiences?

c. "And I would do whatever you ask in my name, so that the Father may be glorified in the Son" (John 14:13). How can we look at the promise of healing and continue trusting God when healing is denied (Proverbs 3:5-6)?

59. Looking Beyond the Mountain of Affliction

a. What affliction looms largest in your life at this present time? How do you view it in the context and perspective of your entire life?

b. How would you describe the mountain you are currently facing?

c. As God meets you during the times of your affliction, how has He refined you in the midst of the affliction? How is God presently etching his image into the fabric of your life?

60. Seasoned

a. Recall a mountaintop experience you have had. What about a deep valley experience? How did you respond in the seasons of these events? In what ways did they season your walk with the Lord?

b. What kind of day has it been for you today? How has God assured you that his eyes are upon you?

c. If the mountains and valleys "drink the rain from heaven," how might you view your times in either place with this in mind? What has kept you nourished as you recall many of your days?

About the Author

Lynn Severance graduated in 1965 from the University of Washington with a BA in elementary education. During her twenty-seven-year teaching career, Lynn wrote curriculum for her school district and the state of Washington. Seattle's PBS television studios were her classroom for two years as she co-wrote and co-produced two series of programs used in the Washington State schools. Two of those twenty-seven years were spent on the East Coast: one year working in Washington, D.C. as part of the VISTA program and a second year working back in the classroom teaching.

She represented her school district on curriculum committees and at national conventions. Since 1980, she has been a member of Alpha Delta Kappa, an international honorary organization for women educators. She has served in various offices at the local and state levels. In 1990 she received their annual Living Memorial Scholarship awarded for the purpose of travel to create classroom curriculum.

In 1983, a one-time intense vertigo attack left Lynn with permanent vestibular dysfunction resulting in constant dizziness, intermittent sessions of internal vertigo attacks, related side effects of nausea, tenuous balance, neck and back pain, visual tracking challenges and constant fatigue. Thoroughly evaluated with many therapies attempted, this condition remains unresolved. She continued teaching with joy for nine years, God directing every move and helping her adapt.

In 1987, she underwent surgery for what turned out to be an aggressive form of breast cancer, discovered early, but requiring six months of follow-up chemotherapy.

In 1992 she embraced an unexpected early retirement option with a retirement goal to write in the genre of inspirational non-fiction. She was included in 1992's *Who's Who Among America's Teachers,* nominated by her former first and third grade student, Mark Myers, who graduated from high school that same year.

Lynn's writing goals came slowly as she could not use a typewriter or look at a computer screen without going into vertigo attacks. That took a positive turn in 2000 by God's grace, the gift of a used computer, and a period of months carefully desensitizing to be able to compensate for the screen's flickering and her visual tracking challenges. She works at a small laptop screen, lying on a couch, pillows cushioning her head to lessen some of the internal fighting against the dizziness.

Writing devotionals for Rest Ministries emerged in 2008, three years after a failed neurological vestibular "healing plan" resulted in a severe time of limitations and being homebound. It has taken some years, but Lynn has been able to cautiously get involved in activities outside the home again. Having been able to travel prior to this setback, she continues to "travel the world" by meeting, ministering, and being encouraged by many online encounters! This book is a result of those travels and the years that came before them. Lynn lives in Lynnwood, Washington, a city just north of Seattle.

Contact Information

To order additional copies of this book,
either in print or E-book format, please visit
www.redemption-press.com

Or call toll free 1-844-2REDEEM.

Bulk order copies (10 or more) are available at the Redemption Press Book Store at a 15%
discount or call Redemption Press directly at 844-273-3336 (844-2REDEEM).

A free PDF downloadable copy of the book's Study Guide, with spaces
for written responses, is available on Lynn's website.

Spirited Comfort
(www.lynnseverance.com)

CPSIA information can be obtained
at www.ICGtesting.com
Printed in the USA
LVIC06n0139111216
516665LV00002B/2